WHY DID IT HAPPEN TO ME

BY

ELGIN DAVIS

authorHOUSE®

AuthorHouse™
1663 Liberty Drive, Suite 200
Bloomington, IN 47403
www.authorhouse.com
Phone: 1-800-839-8640

First published by AuthorHouse 1/12/2009

ISBN: 978-1-4389-0692-8 (sc)
ISBN: 978-1-4389-0693-5 (hc)

Printed in the United States of America
Bloomington, Indiana

This book is printed on acid-free paper.

www.ElginDavis.com

Table of Contents

PREFACE

The completion of this book is a tremendous blessing and one of life's greatest accomplishments. This book solidified my purpose, and I'll never forget this unique and cultivating experience. Eighteen years ago on a cool brisk autumn afternoon, I made my way to the top of Diamond Hill Mountain in Cumberland, Rhode Island, that's where I reflected on life's journey. I wondered how I became so successful in spite of insurmountable obstacles forged against me. God delivered me through life's vicissitudes to become a prominent NFL player, minister, husband, father, and a citizen of good will. It was truly an honor introducing the world to my family, especially my mother and father. I never could have become the man I am today without their help and love. Through this book, their memory will never be forgotten, and their spirits shall live on forever.

My prayers speak for the meek and broken hearted, and I sympathize with those that have fallen short along life's journey. Therefore, I offer this book as my gift to you.

To all that have prayed and inspired me with words of encouragement or fasted as a token of human sacrifice for God's acceptance of this book, I thank you from the bottom of my heart. Words are just not adequate to express my deepest gratitude.

ACKNOWLEDGMENTS

First, I'd like to give God all the glory and honor for blessing me so abundantly. This book is dedicated to my mother, Azalene James, and my father, Fred Davis, my grandparents, Jeadie Davis, Daddy Joe, and Momma Mae. To my Aunts and Uncles in Jesup, especially Vern Gibbs, who always treated me like her son. To my cousins, thanks Jackie for teaching me how to catch my first baseball. Lenny, thank you for the wisdom that you imparted with me; I could have never made it without you. Jack and Oretha Jackson, thanks for being there for both my father and grandmother. To Brother Alvin Mitchell, I love you so much for who you are. I will never forget the love and patience that you demonstrated to my dad; you are truly an angel. To Nancy Bellas and Valerie Fuqua, thank you for being a friend in a time of need. To my sister Stacy James and my nephew Ahmad, I carry your hopes and dreams deeply in my heart. To Reverend Charles Dailey and family, thanks for your inspiration and prayers. To my friends

Jack Johnson, Vernon Wheeler, and Darryl Usher, thank you for the precious memories that you left behind and those that are yet to come. To Kirt Mitchell, thank you for your guidance and support of this project. To my ex-wife Renita, I thank you for giving me two beautiful daughters, Angelica and Yasmeen. To Joe and Hazel Reed, thank you for your unconditional love and support. Thank you Felicia for giving me Myka and sharing Stephen. Thanks Veronique for sharing your heart; the memories shall live forever. To Emma, thanks for helping to nurture me into the man that I am today; your love will always be felt. To my dear friend and angel Allison Pate, words are inadequate to express my appreciation for your unyielding sacrifice and support. Thanks for being a shoulder to cry on, but most of all thanks for being a good listener. You are truly a blessing, and your spirit shall live within me forever. And finally to Minister Farrakhan, thank you for introducing me to Islam and exemplifying the greatest example of humility, sacrifice, and love of God.

INTRODUCTION

Night fall was rapidly approaching as I began my ascent to the mountain peak of Diamond Hill. I was extremely careful, making sure not to twist an ankle or knee while navigating the uneven mountainous terrain. I found the beautiful colors of autumn unparallel to anything I had ever seen. The voices of nature suspended me momentarily in time along the virgin hillsides. Powerful northern winds blew angrily as leaves and twigs rained down from heaven. Slowly, I made my way up the mountain's summit. That's when I finally realized just how far in life I had climbed. I reminisced about the days of old that took me back to those special events and loved ones that made life truly worth living.

It was a unique time in history when revolutionary ideas changed the complexion of America. Blacks became an integral part of the social fabric; especially in the South where images of shame and ridicule were slowly being replaced by self-respect and love. The black church and the soulful sounds of old negro spirituals strengthened our faith through the hardest of times. The voices of Malcolm and Martin championed our cause for freedom, justice, and equality. We were black and proud! Blacks were owning homes and businesses, and a piece of the American dream was becoming as common as fried chicken and collard greens. It was the fabulous sixties. Afros, bell bottoms, and drive-in movies were the talk of the town, and teenagers twisted to the sounds of Chubby Checker. The engagement of war in Vietnam divided our nation. Nevertheless, John F. Kennedy charismatically won the hearts of the American people. He earned the respect and love of poor people just like us. Heck, we even sent a man to the moon for the very first time.

Those were some of the memories that made the sixties so special. But the greatest thing about the sixties occurred October 23, 1965; because that's the day I was born. And from that moment on, the world has never been the same...and this is my story!

SECTION I: DAWN

My parents, Fred and Azalene, were simple folks with hearts as pure as gold. My father was a rare gem, and his true beauty was unlaced by his glowing charm. My grandfather's untimely death forced him to assume the daily responsibilities of manhood at the tender age of thirteen. Daddy attended the funeral draped in his father's suit, and he stuffed his shoes with cardboard to cover the holes. Dad worked a paper route

after school to help pay bills. His mother was a strong black woman that represented freedom and independence. She didn't believe in living in debt, because it led to slavery and oppression. The only person that she was in debt to was God. My grandmother (J) was a tall, fair skinned woman, with curly black hair and Native American features. She was a woman of the earth, a farm girl. When I was a little boy, I helped her grow vegetables in the garden. During spring we harvested fruits and vegetables for lunch and dinner. When we were in need of household items, J hitched a ride from someone going in the direction of her favorite store. Day Light was a rundown grocery store that was nestled in the heart of the ghetto. The store catered to selling cheap food, like pig tail and neck bones, which accommodated the needs of the poor. J's uncontrollable crave for wild and exotic food became a tradition that authenticated her heritage. She'd jump over two cows to catch a possum! To earn

extra money she'd wash clothes and cook meals for the local labor men. We were the first black family on the block to own a home. Nevertheless, daddy was constantly chased by neighborhood bullies. But J was hard and stern. She demanded that he fight back and defend himself by any means necessary.

Dad's true love was basketball, but his hopes of playing in the NBA were drenched in sorrow after sustaining a devastating knee injury. Dad slid into the gym wall and ripped his knee into shreds. It was a tragic injury to say the least. My father had an undeniable spirit to excel. He practiced shooting tin cans at night, and swam during the day to

rehabilitate his knee. Remarkably, he returned and reclaimed his starting position. Heroically, he received a standing ovation and became Stanton's most acclaimed player. As an athlete, I embraced his passion, and giving up was never an option. Dad taught me how to overcome difficulty by having the right attitude and determination.

My mom was one of eight children from a small country town in Georgia. Most of the town's residents were blue collar workers. They believed in keeping life simple and easy. My mother's parents were share croppers; they raised hogs and chickens to make ends meet. Often, we'd travel to the family farm in Surrency to butcher a hog. The process was ruthless. Uncle Waymon loaded his double barrel shotgun and fired at the hog at close range. Blood splattered and stained our garments. Scolding hot water was poured onto the carcass to remove the hair. Skillfully, Uncle Waymon butchered the carcass and divided it among the family. Momma Mae bid for the most delectable part, the intestines. It was considered a delicacy; we called them chitterlings.

During the summer, I'd run bare-foot, and play hide and go seek with my cousins on the rich clay roads until I passed out! I don't think life could've gotten any better! Back in those days, blacks lived in little tin-roof shot-gun houses with cracks between the floor boards; you could even see rats running underneath. During the winter we nearly froze, and during summer we burned up, but no one complained. Back in those days no one feared being hurt or harmed. At night, we slept with our windows open and our doors unlocked. Each man was his brother's keeper. Getting credit at the corner store until payday was never a problem because a mans word was more precious than gold. The lessons I learned from those experiences proved to be monumental in developing my character.

Mom and Auntie moved to Jacksonville in the early sixties to attend Walkers College, that's where she met dad. Their irresistible passion for each other culminated into mom giving birth to me on a cool autumn day. Daddy envisioned me playing basketball, and named me after his favorite player. Elgin Baylor was a dazzling performer for the LA Lakers. Unfortunately, dad's precarious lifestyle led to excessive drinking, and it forged an insurmountable wedge in their relationship. Consequently, I bore the brunt of his pain and suffering, and it shaped my destiny. Dad stopped working and hung out at the local bars and pool hall. On rare occasions, he'd take me to my doctor visits while mom worked. The women thought that it was cute, especially when he'd pin my diaper up wrong. Often, dad snuck me into the local night clubs to meet the celebrities that entertained in town. Those little clubs later became known as the "chitterling circuit" because blacks weren't allowed to perform in major venues. One of those entertainers was Jackie Wilson. He autographed my first baby picture. There were others like David Ruffin of the Temptations. As I grew older, I overheard dad talking about David Ruffin. He had a terrible drug addiction, and was found tragically murdered. However, dad was most impressed meeting Dr. Martin Luther King, his wife Coretta, and their children. Dad was admired by everybody, he had a magnetic personality. However, he became an alcoholic and remained unemployed for eleven years. Dad was loud and rambunctious. He preferred hanging out in the streets and was well equipped for the urban lifestyle.

Mom worked odd jobs to keep food on the table. Soon she moved out and got an apartment on Flag Street; it was a desirable location for blacks. Dad's condition gradually worsened. One day J sent me to the bar to get daddy for dinner. I saw him lying in the ditch drunk. My heart dropped and felt so much love for him. I said in a tender voice, "Come on daddy get up. It's time to go eat." Even at the age of five, I reserved the best interests of my daddy at heart. I helped him to his feet. We struggled and staggered home down the hopeless streets of despair, while kids stared and laughed. Learning how to love and sacrifice came at an early age, but not without a price to be paid.

As a kid I played recklessly. I had no fear; I was a dare-devil to say the least. Often, I'd jeopardize my safety with foolish stunts. Mom's heart nearly faltered as she'd rescue me from the ledge of our third floor balcony. A loss of balance would have sent me plummeting several stories onto the concrete below. The consequences would've been catastrophic. However, my greatest thrill was fishing with daddy's poles. I had a vivid imagination; dad's trophies were a perfect catch! Often, I'd tie them to his poles and reel them up to the balcony. Dad's presence was always welcome, as I yelled, "Look daddy, I caught a big one!" He'd smile and shake his head.

My best friend was Danny, he lived downstairs. We'd play until I heard dad call me just before sunset. I'd run full speed and wouldn't stop until I jumped into my daddy's arms. I followed dad inside and listened while his singing group, The Four Counts, drank liquor and mimicked the Temptations.

Later that year, mom and dad separated, but she was determined to survive. Before work, she'd walk miles in the blistering heat with me on her shoulders. Thirsty and fatigued, mom straggled into the house. Before rushing off to work, J poured her a cool drink. J taught me the secrets of the land. Her name was Jeadie, but it was hard for me to pronounce; I called her J. On many crisp autumn nights I sat on the floor next to J, while she pealed purple sticks with a butcher knife. She made sure to spread newspaper over the floor to catch the peelings as they dropped. I'll never forget the way J smacked, as juice dripped down her chin. It wasn't long before I was smacking on those purple sticks with her; I loved them. Later, I found out those sticks were called sugar cane.

Many nights, mom was late picking me up and I'd sit in a corner and weep until I heard J's comforting voice say, "Don't cry, it's alright your momma's coming." I loved my mother with all my heart. Often, I waited in front of the gate hoping to catch a glimpse of her. When she arrived, I ran quickly and jumped into her arms. I told my mom that when she died, I wanted to die with her. I had a special bond with my mom and dad. J always sent me home with a good meal; she loved cooking. I miss those days very much. That was thirty five years ago, but I remember it like it was yesterday.

Eventually, mom had had enough and divorced daddy. She remarried a preacher, Joseph James. Lenny was his middle name and that's what I called him. Lenny appeared to be a genius; he knew everything. He was a self-educated man that read a lot. He made a good living as a long shore-man and life was more comfortable. Mom's walking days were over. While enjoying a family outing, I challenged Lenny's authority with barbaric behavior. He bent over to retrieve an item and I kicked him in the ass! Mom was embarrassed. She placed her hand over her mouth and screamed, "No! Elgin no!" Bystanders looked astounded while Lenny and mom scolded me. The silly grin on my face quickly disappeared with the presence of Lenny's belt.

The next day was a horrific memory that pierced my heart. As mom and I drove Lenny to work, we passed the bar where dad hung out. We stopped at the traffic light. Daddy was sitting on the sidewalk drunk and dirty. However, he held his head up high with dignity and pride, so did I. We stared into each other's eyes and waved until we faded away into the horizon; it was a painful experience that haunts me to this day.

I was seven years old when we moved into our new house. It had a pool and a lake in the backyard. I loved fishing in the lake for bass and brim. I didn't have a fishing pole, just a string and hook. I caught all the fish I wanted. Quickly, I learned the patterns of the lake. In the early morning, the brim fed on live worms and bread. However, it was much harder catching fish in the heat of the day. In late evening, right before sunset, the lake was at its best! Not only did I catch brim, but also bass and catfish. The lake became my second home.

On some occasions, I swam in the lake. Momma was afraid of the hidden dangers that lurked beneath, so I stopped. Growing up as an only child was lonely. However, I considered myself extremely lucky because I had the greatest mom in the world. She made sure that I had a nutritious meal, clean clothes, and a bath at night. When mom walked into the bathroom, I made sure to cover up; I was beginning to feel uncomfortable. That was a clear sign that I was growing up. However, a part of me enjoyed being a child, especially playing in the tub with my toys. When I finished bathing, it was time for dinner. Exotic food wasn't on the menu; Lenny preferred traditional meals. I was being groomed to fit perfectly in society. From this experience, I learned how to live a diverse lifestyle; it became an integral part of my foundation.

Every night mom braided my hair. She didn't like it packed down and nappy. I'll never forget the night mom forgot to braid my hair. The next morning, she straightened my hair with a hot comb until all the kinks were out. When she got close to the edge, she'd say, "Be still, I don't want to burn you." I didn't twitch a muscle.

Minutes later, I had an instant blow out! In those days, whoever had the most hair became popular. The competition was steep, especially at an all black school. Well, mom had run out of conditioner, and my hair was dry and brittle. She did the unthinkable, and went to the refrigerator and got the chicken grease from dinner the night before. We were used to improvising, but never like that! To make a long story short, my hair was no longer dry and brittle; it was perfect! However, all the kids in school were sniffing during class saying, "Ya'll smell chicken?" Adjusting to circumstances became a way of life in order to survive. Sometimes, we even had to dry our clothes in the oven. The worst thing was forgetting to take them out in time, and having to wear burnt socks and underwear to school. When we couldn't afford gas and had no way of cooking we turned the iron upside down and cook on top of it. That was unfortunate, but back then it was just a part of life. We were happy regardless of the circumstances; to this day, mom and I chuckle.

My new school was close to home, and it saved mom lots of time and money. She didn't have to drop me off and pick me up in the afternoon. However, there was one problem, I was home alone. Mom had no choice but to leave me alone until she got home from work; that terrified her. To avoid danger, obedience became essential. I wasn't permitted to leave the house or let anyone in. Mom told me that if anyone rang the doorbell not to answer. That's exactly what I did for many years.

Being alone never bothered me, I found peace within myself. When I got hungry I ate, when I got sleepy I slept. However, mom never allowed me to go swimming without a grown up because I didn't know how to swim. The thought of me drowning was her greatest fear.

The thing I loved about my family was that we never went to bed without praying together; that was instilled in me at an early age. It became the foundation of my spirituality and the secret behind my success throughout life. Being a year older, I was granted permission to visit friends in the neighborhood. My first friend was Tim. He lived across the street. What I remember most about Tim is his chubby belly and charming smile. My other friend was Bernard. He loved fishing in the lake with me. He showed me a lot of fishing tricks I still use today. The last time I checked, Bernard still lived in that house. Also, he was up to those same fishing tricks.

Later that week, something miraculous happened that changed my life. I'll never forget that night, as I knelt on my knees and prayed. I was transformed by the Holy Spirit and formed an intimate relationship with the Lord. After eating dinner, I recall mom and Lenny saying goodnight and tucking me into bed. I drifted into a deep state of meditation. Energy and power intruded my body. A voice from within spoke to me saying, "God." The voice was rich and powerful. Terrified, I jumped up looking around. In a panic, I ran to mom's room, finding her and Lenny sound asleep. Lenny was snoring. The spirit told me not to be afraid. I went back to my room and finished my prayers. I never heard that voice again, but that was the beginning of many spiritual phenomena's that I can't explain. That experience changed my life, and I knew that God was real.

The next week I celebrated my ninth birthday. Tim and a couple of other friends stopped by. Dad didn't make it to my party, he was struggling to overcome the effects of alcohol; yet I knew he loved me. Nevertheless, I had a great party and felt very special.

Later I went to see J. Dad was sitting in his car drunk; he had a blue Pontiac Bonneville with no tires. It sat on cement blocks. Poor dad was slumped inside with the engine running and his foot on the pedal. I could hear the engine roaring from far away. No one could make him stop, not even me. J requested the church elders to come over and pray for him. Daddy went crazy, and knocked a gaping hole in the wall.

They said, "Fred, you got to give your life to Jesus."

Daddy screamed, "Fuck Jesus!"

The elders began speaking in tongues, as tears raced from their eyes. They begged God's forgiveness and anointed his head with oil. I was terrified; it ruptured my soul. But, I was being groomed for a special mission. Sometimes, daddy disappeared for days, but we always knew where to find him (Cherry's Bar).

For the holidays, mom and I went to Georgia and exchanged gifts. We reminisced about the old days, while eating dinner. What I remember most was prayer time. We all stood around the kitchen table staring at enough food to feed a village! Momma Mae led the prayer; she was the glue that kept the family together. Then, each person around the table would recite a short bible verse. At that time I didn't know one. When it was my turn they skipped me.

The fresh scent of pine fumigated the house, and the Christmas tree was decorated with silver and gold. Sometimes, I helped mom wrap the presents, and the thought of Ole St. Nick loomed larger than life. Auntie Vern was like a second mom; she never had kids. She showered me with gifts, and treated me like her own. Mom made sure I had a gift under the tree for my family; that always drew big smiles from them.

Growing up in two households gave me balance and a different perspective of life. As wonderful as the holidays were, there was one major drawback. Dad drank more alcohol. As I matured, dad's drinking was harder for me to accept. Sometimes he'd vomit and make strange moans; it gave me the creeps.

At times, he'd say in a slurred voice, "Who's your daddy?"

I answered in a soft, humble voice, "You are daddy."

"What's my name boy?" He demanded that I hold my head up while speaking. He was lost and in big trouble.

Mom and Lenny never belittled dad. They encouraged me to respect him and to remain being a humble child. I loved them for that. Mom asked if I wanted to call Lenny dad. But I was proud of my father, and I loved him immensely in spite of his infirmities. I told mom no.

The stress of growing up had a cumulative effect. As a result, I was an unaccomplished student to say the least, and my progress was impeded by a substandard educational system. I struggled helplessly from grade to grade. As I grew older, I was delegated more chores; I hated it. But Lenny gave me something that would last a lifetime, discipline! I thought that he was mean because he had to speak firm in order to gain my attention. His tactics appeared harsh, but it was effective. Discipline proved to be the overwhelming quality that sustained my growth. Lenny helped me to understand things from a Biblical prospective; he shaped me into a young man. Mom supplied a mixture of tenderness and mercy; I was changing overnight. My foundation was laid.

During my leisure time, I played basketball in the park with Barry and Reginal Lester. Instinctively, I inclined towards Barry; he was much older and fairly short for his age. He told me his parents sold honey drippers at their house; that's frozen cool aid in a cup.

The next day I went to Barry's house to buy a honey dripper. Timidly, I walked towards the front door and knocked. I was set at ease when I heard a sweet, gentle voice reply, "Yes, may I help you?"

Staring into her eyes, I paused and said, "Do you have any honey drippers?"

She responded with a smile and asked, "What size?"

I reached into pocket and handed her a quarter. She returned with a gigantic honey dripper. My eyes lit up; I was thrilled! Immediately, I pasted my lips against the cup and began sucking. That's when a tall, dark skinned man appeared from nowhere. Slowly, he walked towards me with a grim look on his face. With his arm extended, he firmly shook my hand and introduced himself as Coach Cook, the head football coach for the Forest View Trojans. He asked me my name and if I wanted to play football. With my knees and hands trembling, emphatically, I shouted, "Yes!"

Mrs. Cook requested my parents name and number, and told me to go home and ask my parents. I dropped my honey dripper and dashed home before sunset. I ran in the door yelling, "Ma! Ma! Can I play football?"

Momma was afraid I'd get hurt and didn't take a liking to the idea. She left the decision up to Lenny. He felt that playing football was a great idea, and would teach me many valuable life skills.

Mom said, "But Lenny."

Lenny said, "He'll be alright!"

I said, "Yea mom, I'll be alright! Please momma please." I bounced up and down over and over again.

When mom agreed, I ran through the house like a wild man, faking around chairs and stuff.

Lenny said, "Calm down son, calm down."

That was the happiest day of my life. An hour later the phone rang, it was Coach Cook. He and Lenny talked for a while, I stared anxiously.

I couldn't sleep at all that night because practice started the next day. I had no idea what to expect or how to play!

Fortunately, daddy was making progress with his drinking problem, with the help of A.A. and a special woman that changed his life. I grew to love this woman. That relationship proved to be the missing link that brought the family together. Emma shared some of the most exciting memories of my life. When I met her, she was driving a purple Barracuda. She had plenty of kids and grand-kids for me to play with. When I told dad I was playing football, his face lit up like the sun; he was proud. It was the first time that I saw my dad sober; it was pleasing.

The day I had been waiting for had finally arrived, and life as I knew it would never be the same. After school I rode with Barry to practice. I didn't say a word, I was scared. I heard whistles blaring and kids were throwing and kicking footballs, it was chaotic. I didn't know where to go so I followed Barry. When I tried following Barry to his team they told me I was too small. I felt lost without him. Eventually, I made my way over to a group of guys my size. The coach had us all take a knee and he started yelling. I was terrified. When he asked a question, everybody responded by yelling, "Yes sir!" Coach demanded respect. Coach Richardson helped me to appreciate the value of strong leadership.

On the way home I saw daddy and Emma waiting by the gate, I was surprised. He looked great, especially with Emma by his side. That's what I loved about my daddy; he was there to support me from the beginning.

Meanwhile, Lenny became the Assistant Pastor at Macedonia Baptist Church. He inculcated egalitarian principles which molded my faith. But Lenny excluded himself from many of the principles that he taught. Nonetheless, I valued the truth and tried living an exemplary life. Quickly, I established myself as a leader among my peers. Dad also joined the church; he needed God's help and strength to remain sober. The First Baptist of Oakland became our house of worship. Reverend

17

C.B. Dailey became my first spiritual leader, and I grew to love and cherish him. Finally, dad was headed in the right direction.

The next practice I received my football equipment. I didn't know how to put on my uniform; my teammates helped me out. Defense

and offense were strange terms that I had never heard before. My first position was defensive line. I ran wild, tackling guys on my side. My teammates thought that I was crazy. After coach told me what to do, I was really good. Nevertheless, coach changed my position to offensive tackle; I wore #73. I took pride in my position; however, I wasn't the best player. That honor went to our running back Jello; a position that I would master, and make a living performing. Jello was fast, real fast. He was a little chubby for a running back, but when it came to running he had no problem. He scored a lot of touchdowns. That made him popular with the coaches and players, but especially among the cheerleaders.

Dad and Emma sat next to mom and Lenny and cheered at my games. It was encouraging to see everybody together. Their support nurtured my progress. After the season ended, the team had a banquet. There were throngs of people; not an empty seat. I was very nervous.

Mom and Lenny sat with me; we ate as much food as we wanted. One by one each player received a trophy followed by loud applause from the crowd. Then, suddenly Coach Richardson focused directly at us and said these words, "I've been coaching for fifteen years and I have never met a child as special and well mannered as this kid. This is a tribute to you, and your parents, for raising such a fine young man."

Mom and Lenny stood nobly holding hands and joyfully embracing each other. Gently, mom grabbed a napkin and wiped away her tears. Then her eyes sparkled like diamonds and a smile resonated on her face as she watched me receive my first trophy. That's when the audience erupted with a standing ovation. That was the first of many awards I received throughout my life. I wished that daddy was present; he would've been proud.

Meanwhile, daddy found a job at the Standard Feed Company working in the warehouse, bagging feed and grain; it changed his life. Mr. Moore and his brother owned the store. It was in walking distance from J's house. The company had everything from gardening supplies to livestock. In spite of the horrible smell, multitudes patronized the feed store for their gardening supplies. For entertainment, I played with the baby ducks. I made sure that they had plenty of water and food. Dad was admired by many, and I followed him around the store like a shadow. He was proud to inform his friends and coworkers that I played football. Sometimes, Mr. Moore gave me money just for being a good kid.

Dad was living well. He managed his money wisely, and showered himself with simple pleasures. His prized possession was a 1974 Buick Riviera; it was red with a black top. Emma sewed red outfits for him to match his car; he was a sight to see.

Daddy surprised me with a duck from the feed store, I named her Miranda. Since we had a lake over at mom and Lenny's I took her there. While she was a baby, I kept her in a box in my room. I loved that little duck. Daddy gave me a bag of duck feed from the store and when we ran out I gave her bread. It didn't take long for her to grow up. Soon, Miranda was too big for the box so I set her free in the lake. I feared that I'd never see her again.

Every day I walked to the edge of the bank and called her name, "Miranda! Quack, quack, quack!" After about three minutes Miranda would come. I fed her bread, just like when she was a baby, if the fish didn't eat it first. We met like that for years. Later she disappeared. Nevertheless, I continued buying ducks and setting them free for many years.

That year was fun. Dad and Emma explored new expeditions; crabbing was our favorite. There was a special place called the North Side Generating Plant. The water was exceptionally warm and the crabs loved it. We got chicken backs and left them out of the refrigerator for days because the rotten chicken would drive the crabs crazy, and us too. But it worked like a charm. We used basket traps and tied the chicken in the middle and then a brick on the bottom so the tide wouldn't carry the traps away.

The night before, dad and I prepared the cooler and gathered our favorite snacks. He loved eating sardines and crackers and I got candy. Dad and I slept restlessly, and awoke to the smell of freshly brewed coffee. The morning dew slowly evaporated, as crickets chirped under a crescent moon. Dad was eager to hit the road. He jumped into the car and revved the engine. I followed closely behind, and crammed the trunk with our fishing gadgets. Our journey toward the coast was adventurous. The celestial views of the wetlands were a hallmark of beauty. When we arrived, dad found the perfect spot. Sometimes, we trapped a dozen or more crabs; other times maybe three or four. We took naps under the bridge to escape the blistering heat. Afterwards we went to Emma's and invited her family and friends over to eat crabs. Life didn't get any better than that. Daddy was getting stronger day by day. He had stopped drinking liquor, but he found beer irresistible;

Schlitz Malt Liquor Bull was his favorite. At night we'd walk to the Little Brown Jug, a local liquor store on the corner. Daddy purchased two cans of beer. He'd drink one can on the way back home, and save the other. Often, we threw sticks and stones to defend ourselves from vicious predators.

One night, I had a living nightmare that I'll never forget. We all went to sleep early that night. Sometime around 3AM I felt Emma shaking me and heard her say in a panic stricken voice, "Elgin get up, we have to go!"

I sensed something was terribly wrong, and I was right. Dad was lying motionless in a pool of blood. Only the white of his eyes were visible and he had no pulse; he looked dead. I was traumatized. Shortly afterwards, the ambulance arrived and rushed dad to the hospital. Emma and I followed closely behind. I was up all night in the emergency room with Emma waiting for news. That was the worst night of my life. When morning came we talked with the doctor. He said if we had waited any longer, dad would've died. Mom and Emma communicated regularly; they slowly built a friendship. Shortly, dad was released. I gave him a big hug and told him that I loved him. Dad was hurting inside, and I blamed myself.

Two weeks later, daddy was drinking again, despite J's desperate pleas. She cried, "Fred, please stop!"

But he wouldn't.

Emma said, "Fred you know better, are you trying to kill yourself?"

I said nothing and looked at him with a sad face.

Pain and frustration festered within. I was a time bomb waiting to explode. Slowly, I was becoming a victim and showed signs of its effects.

The year had come and gone and it was time for another season. I noticed that I was much smaller than the rest of my teammates. I was playing with guys much older and it showed. I was a tough athlete, and the coach moved me to the left guard to utilize my athletic ability. My number was changed to 63.

One dreary afternoon, I slipped during practice and a host of teammates landed on my arm. I tried to get up but the pain was too intense. I shouted, "My arm, my arm!"

The coaches came running and asked if I could move it. I tried, but couldn't, it was numb and heavy. I looked down at my arm and the bone was protruding.

The coach said, "Don't look down!"

My teammates gathered around grimacing. I tried my best not to cry, but the pain was unbearable. Tears burst from my eyes, and fell like rain. Coach Larry made a sling out of his belt and put my arm in it. Then, we rushed to the hospital. The ride was treacherous. Hitting bumps and pot-holes was unavoidable, and caused the pain to escalate.

Coach said, "Be tough, we're almost there son, we're almost there."

When I got to the hospital it didn't take long to see a doctor. Shortly afterward, mom and Lenny arrived.

Mom was in a frenzy. Lenny said, "He's alright, just be calm."

I shouted in a stern voice, "I'll never play football again." My arm had no feeling.

Gently, mom held my hand. The doctor gave me a shot to kill the pain then started adjusting my arm to reset the fracture. I sat right there and didn't say a word. He wrapped my arm with strips of damp white cloth until it hardened forming a cast; it reached my shoulder. The cast was damp and heavy. That was the first of many tragic injuries that I would endure as an athlete. Dad was very sad to hear about what had happened. I was hoping he wouldn't drink because that was the last thing I needed.

The next day I stayed home from school to get acclimated to my cast, it sucked! Mom butchered the sleeve of my shirts to accommodate my needs. Proudly, I paraded around modeling a unique wardrobe.

J moved a relative into her home from a mental institution in Chattahoochee. Her name was Cousin B; a short middle aged woman. She maintained the chores around the house, including taking care of me. B never said a word, she answered yes ma'am in her sweet southern voice. I guess any place was better than the crazy house. When I fell asleep on the couch she spread a blanket over me. The only thing warmer was her heart. I grew to love B.

When I returned to school the kids signed my cast. My teacher was very patient with me because I had to learn how to write with my left hand. Even back then, I found ways to overcome adversity.

The next day, Lenny took me to the park. Coach stopped practice and all the fellows came running to greet me. They embraced me and signed my cast. I felt like a king. During the games I sat with the team on the bench and helped handing out water.

Dad started drinking again, but not without a price to be paid. He smashed into another car and left the scene. Later, he turned himself in to the police. He was given a citation and his license was suspended. Dad didn't fear anything, not even death. Without a car dad had to walk. One night while walking from the Brown Jug, a pack of vicious dogs tried to attack him. A stray dog defended dad until he made it home. Daddy told me that the dog came in the form of an angel. We named him Major. Ten years passed before daddy took another drink.

With a broken arm there wasn't much to do. That's when I received the perfect gift, an electronic football set. I played for hours alone in my room. I had a captive imagination. I announced the players like an actual sports commentator and kept stats on each player. I even had a banquet. I made the trophies from aluminum foil.

It was 1976 and mom was pregnant with my sister, Stacy. This made me angry, probably because I was the only child for so long and I was used to getting attention. Mom and Lenny's marriage was turbulent and they argued a lot. It made me sad. Lenny yelled and said a lot of bad words to momma. She cried all the time. Sometimes Lenny disappeared, leaving us alone for hours late into the night. Mom suffered many complications and needed medicine from the store to relieve the pain; her stomach hurt a lot. I walked miles to the store for her.

I remember momma saying to me, "Son, please rub momma's stomach."

My mother represented the greatest attributes of all, humility and mercy, that I inherited. As I grew older, I forgave those who persecuted us. I was inspired to pray through troubled times, and I vowed never to mistreat a woman when I got married. Mom always remained vivacious no matter how bad things got. She gave me a good example of what a woman stood for. Thank you momma!

When Stacy was born a lot changed. I had to help out more around the house, warm the baby's bottle and get diapers. Sometimes mom would let me feed her. I enjoyed being a big brother.

It was time for the cast to come off; that was great news. The next day momma took me to see the doctor. He pulled out something that resembled a saw and cut right through the cast. The room smelled like smoke. When the doctor removed the cast my arm had a bad odor and was tiny.

He felt around my arm and said, "It's all healed and looks good. Be careful and take it easy."

We rushed over to surprise J. I ran into the house screaming, "Look J, look!" That was a happy day, she was thrilled. Daddy gave me a small rubber ball to squeeze to strengthen my arm.

However, without football I felt lost. To fill the void I joined the band. I played the violin. I practiced day and night until I became great. The noise must have driven mom and Lenny insane.

Sometimes mom cried out, "It's too loud son, you're going to wake up the baby!"

Instead, I went outside and woke up the neighbors. I became an accomplished student.

Girls became my next interest; there were two in particular. It started with passing notes in class. I was growing up.

Dad had saved enough money to buy another car; it was a canary yellow Riviera. He even opened an account at the Young Men Shop and bought all kinds of fancy clothes. He used to like to wear his shirts unbuttoned with his stomach out, and a panama hat tilted to one side. He was sharp and doing well, probably because the Lord had entered into his life. Daddy became a different man. I was so proud of him; he became the dad I always wanted. Daddy quoted the sayings of great men and instilled a belief in me that I could reach the top. He made me feel special. He encouraged me to do my best and never give up, and that's what I did regardless of the circumstances. It would take my best to fulfill my dreams.

I went to J's every other weekend. On Sundays I went to church with dad at the First Baptist of Oakland. We sat in the same spot each

week. I enjoyed the preaching. There was something about the word that moved my spirit. After church, J delighted in cooking big meals. When J wasn't cooking or watching the Mike Douglas Show, she sat at the dinner table dipping snuff with her spit can nearby. She'd place her false teeth in a glass and read the newspaper. She usually listened to the church service on the radio because she was having trouble walking. Old age and arthritis slowly crept into her knees and hands limiting her mobility.

Football season was here again. This time I dropped down to the Forest View Blazers with guys my own age and size. Freddie Stephens was our coach. Playing with the older guys prepared me to be mentally and physically superior. I was a man playing among boys. I decided to play running back. From that day forward I never played another position again. Quickly, I discovered I had a natural God given talent; the coaches were astonished. Back with the Trojans I thought Jello was good; however, no one had perfected their craft as skillfully as Rollie Scott. Bootney was his nickname and he stood every bit of 4'4". He was almost the size of a midget. Once he scored thirteen touchdowns, in one game! Bootney and I became the starting running backs that year. Dad was extremely proud.

However, I suffered a peculiar foot injury. Emma tried massaging it with a home remedy to relieve the pain; sometimes it worked, and sometimes it didn't. At night, I'd model my uniform in front of the mirror and practice end zone dances. The next morning, I was up bright and early. Mom prepared breakfast and gathered my uniform.

Dad, Emma, mom, and Lenny sat with Bootney's parents at the games. When I made a good play, dad would stand and yell, "That's my son!"

In spite of an injury plagued season, I was voted the team's most outstanding player.

One Saturday night, I watched a movie about two courageous football players, Gale Sayers and Brian Piccolo. Gale Sayers was an electrifying player, and was later inducted into the NFL Hall of Fame; I wanted to be like him. Brian Piccolo's fate ended in tragedy. He died from cancer at the age of twenty-six. Brian's Song infused my heart, and left an everlasting impression. I credit Gale Sayers for inspiring me with ambition to play in the NFL. To honor his legacy I chose to wear #40.

The next morning, I wrote Chicago Bears Here I Come on the back of my door! Over the next ten years, I read those words before going to bed at night. Mom and Lenny weren't too happy about me writing on the door, but they let it stay. That day, Gale Sayers became my idol. My perception of athletics altered the outcome of my life. I even tried playing baseball. The first day of practice I hit a homerun. Everyone was shocked, especially Coach Frank, he threw his best pitch! Despite being terrified of the ball, I was a great left fielder, and catching fly balls was my specialty.

The following year I was bussed to an integrated school miles away; many of my friends attended. Ocean Way Junior High was the largest school that I'd attended. Throngs of students littered the campus, I was nervous. Mr. Farris comforted me; he was my science teacher and the basketball coach. Coach Farris encouraged me to try out. I had reservations but he assured me that I could do it. I trusted him, he was a like a brother. Soon, my faith was rewarded because I made the team.

A couple of weeks later I was introduced to my best friend. I loved Jack Johnson the moment we met. Also, I met Lynn Mitchner; she made my heart flutter. Sometimes I carried her books as we walked to class.

Then the unthinkable happened, she kissed me with her tongue; my toes curled! The rumor accelerated around campus.

Meanwhile, the basketball team prepared to play. I cheered from the sidelines. Basketball didn't come easy, but I tried my best. I scored two points in the final game. I excelled academically; sometimes recording perfect exams. Mrs. Campbell gave me letters of accomplishment; I stood while being recognized.

I looked forward to visiting dad on the weekends, he was doing great. He saved the tips he received in a shoe box located in the closet. It wasn't much, but it quickly added up. My weekends were quickly absorbed; leaving was difficult. J's favorite response was, "So long Joe, so long." I never knew why she called me Joe.

While driving back home daddy played his favorites, Jackie Wilson and Sam Cooke. He always left me with a positive message and eight dollars for my allowance.

Teenagers flocked into sanctuaries, none treasured more than Skate City. Some weekends mom took me there. The urge to smoke and drink alcohol became irresistible to some; mom warned me to beware. I avoided confrontation. However, unpredictable forces hindered my progress.

One day I got into a fight with the school bully. It started in the locker room when someone pushed us into each other. Sam punched my face. Discombobulated, I grabbed and bit him; puncture wounds inflamed his cheek. His face looked horrible. He was rushed to the hospital to get a tetanus shot.

Later, I bit another guy. This time it was Theodore. Soon, everybody got the message to leave me alone. Meanwhile, Jack went on a slapping vengeance when being teased. After a couple of slaps they left him alone too! I guess they also got the message.

Finally, dad had earned vacation and won a trip to Fairfield Mountain in Asheville, North Carolina. I was impregnated with joy! Getting prepared was exciting and invigorating. Dad had a couple of hundred dollars saved, his generosity never ceased. He bought me a tape of Parliament to enjoy on the road. While driving, daddy asked Emma if she had the reservation for the resort. She looked in her purse with a crazy look on her face, I knew something was wrong. Emma had forgotten the reservation. It appeared our vacation was over before it started. Before returning to Jacksonville to retrieve the reservation, dad and Emma argued for nearly two hundred miles.

After retrieving the reservation, we wasted no time in hitting the road. Hours later we arrived in Claxton, Georgia to see Emma's son. We were accosted with love! Roger and his wife built a beautiful home nestled in a cul-de-sac; they even had a basketball goal. Dad and I played until we were exhausted. The adults drank and partied, but dad refused to take a sip; I was very proud of him.

Early the next morning we said goodbye. We hit the road, and anticipated arriving in Asheville around noon. Dad cruised through the red hills of Georgia with the air conditioning cranked up, listening to Jackie Wilson and Sam Cooke. Together, we harmonized the lyrics, before stopping in South Carolina to buy peaches. I craved their succulent taste, and devoured them one by one.

We fled from South Carolina, heading towards the rolling hills. As we approached Asheville, our ears popped and the clouds descended. We knew it wouldn't be long; the signs were all around us! Suddenly, we took a sharp dive, and everything seemed to have vanished. Dad accelerated up the steep road. As we reached the peak, we had a pristine view of the Smokey Mountains. They were breathtaking! Daddy reduced his speed and glanced at the map; the resort was only miles away.

With a litany of majestic trees, flowers, and warm smiles, the resort was a paradise away from home. We had a fully furnished condo on the golf course. The greatest sensation was absorbing the sounds of the waterfalls at night; it was fabulous! The trip was good for dad's self-esteem and our relationship. Just to think, a year ago dad didn't have a car or a job; he was an alcoholic! God is good! I witnessed his power and glorified his name. He was grooming me for a unique journey that would require this example.

After checking in, we cruised down into the valley searching for food, fun, and entertainment. That's when we were lured into a pet store and I discovered a Burmese Python. I approached without trepidation.

Dad said in a nervous voice, "Don't get too close son."

The manager assured me that the snake wouldn't bite. He asked if I wanted to hold him.

I said, "Yes."

He hoisted the snake around my neck! Dad ran out of the store.

Emma shouted, "Be careful!"

The next morning we had an appointment to tour the property. We loved everything about it. They even tried to sell us a vacation home, but we couldn't afford it. I was sad, and I prayed that someday God would bless me to buy my parents the desires of their hearts. But until then, I'd have to wait.

Finally, business was over and it was time to have fun. Driving through the mountains was a daunting task. Narrow winding roads posed an immediate danger, and it demanded our attention. Firmly, dad griped the steering wheel, and drove cautiously until we had safely reached our destination. Chimney Rock was Asheville's most popular tourist attraction. We were intrigued by an array of fascinating crafts and innovations. Our voyage to the summit began when a young maverick guided us to an elevator, through a dark and dismal tunnel. Cautiously, we entered one by one. Suddenly, we were launched twenty-six stories through the core of the mountain. We arrived in a gift shop that overlooked the valley. The view was spectacular!

Our journey to the summit was arduous. Skillfully, we navigated around jagged boulders and steep turns. The sound of the roaring falls guided us to the summit. Hot and fatigued, dad and I retrieved a cool drink of water. The mist gently landed on our face, offering relief from the heat and humidity. With nightfall approaching, we aborted our expedition and headed back.

The next morning we packed and headed home; our trip had come to an end. I reminisced about Asheville, and wished our stay had been longer. While driving, we decided to go to Disney World. I thought about mom and how it would have been nice if she could have seen the beautiful sights in North Carolina. I always wanted to share special memories with the people I loved most. I thank God for that quality of heart.

Finances were nearly depleted; we had to spend wisely. Emma had a daughter Ronnie that lived in Orlando. We had a place to stay. Orlando was exciting with plenty of things to do. Ronnie's husband Miller got us free tickets to Disney. We had never been to Disney and we had no idea of how to dress. We played it safe and put on our Sunday best. We rode to the entrance, an amalgamation of cultures infiltrated the park; it was spectacular!

It was a hot, muggy day. Dressed in our Sunday clothes we were drenched in sweat. We stood in line nearly an hour to ride on <u>2000 Leagues Under the Sea</u>. Suddenly, a roller coaster came racing our way splashing water. We screamed while water dripped from our face. We enjoyed the rides until nightfall.

Disney was beautiful that night. The castle was lit up; there must have been a million lights! Then came the Main Street electrical parade.

I looked at dad as he ate and watched the characters in the parade go by singing these words, "This is the time, this is the place, this is the best time of your life!" Those characters left an everlasting impression on us. Sometimes, I find myself singing that same song today; it really was the best time of our lives!

Soon, our vacation was over, and it was time to head home. Sentimental thoughts made saying goodbye grievous. I reminisced about the mountains, the park, the words we spoke, and the moments of silence. We shared an inner peace that would last a lifetime. I will forever be in debt to God. Sharing time with dad gave me something I would never be able to repay.

I was anxious to see momma, I wanted to tell her all about our vacation. Later that day, daddy drove me home. We hugged, tears rolled from our eyes; no one wanted to say goodbye. We loved each other so much. Daddy didn't know what he had done for me. Somehow I felt that he wanted to share those exact thoughts with me. I treasured those memories. Despite dad's absence, when thinking about our vacation his spirit would always visit me.

After I left dad that night, I felt like a new person. The timing couldn't have been better because it was time for football practice. I was bigger and faster. I had won the hearts of everyone and earned their respect as a player. I started the season right where I left off the year before, toss right and toss left. I scored thirteen touchdowns that year.

One game we were trailed by a touchdown and were about to tie the score. Our quarterback threw me a short pass across the middle, and I dropped it! I could've scored a touchdown. Minutes later, we tried the same play, and I dropped the ball again! That was the worst feeling of my life. Dad was in the stands, and he felt my pain. After the game, I went up in the stands and cried on his shoulders like a baby. My teammates came around to comfort me, some of them cried with me. That day we grew up and learned that failure was a part of success!

Dad said, "You can't win them all son, just get them next week!"

Dad always knew what to say. I took his advice and got them the next week. The next team we played was the 3W Rattlers. They were the best team in Jacksonville, Jack played line-backer. He was known for knocking people out. Jack was an oversized kid that resembled a grown man! Back then, most of the guys were afraid to play the Rattlers. I really had to be a leader. Otherwise, we would have been crushed. The first play of the game I took a hand-off up the middle and ran 88 yards for a touchdown. That was the longest run ever given up by the Rattlers. However, the Rattlers won the game. I think we left the game with the Rattler's respect. But most importantly, the respect from our coaches and each other. Later that year, I won the outstanding offensive player award, while Ronnie took the MVP. I envied the choice, it should have been me. Daddy told me to keep my head up.

My next adventure was running track. Dad took me to Charlie Coleman's to buy track shoes. He was always there for me; I could depend on dad no matter what.

My friend Jack joined the team too. Finally, we were playing with each other instead of against each other. Jack didn't have track shoes, so he borrowed mine. Jack struggled running track, but he always gave it his best. During one track meet at Butler Jr., I ran the 220 against one of the fastest guys in town. When the gun sounded I took the lead. I was always the first out of the blocks, I had a quick start. Somewhere around the curb he regained the lead, it looked as if I didn't have a prayer. Suddenly, I hit another gear and ran him down! That day I won my first race.

Daddy was jumping up and down screaming, "That's my son! That's my son!"

There couldn't have been a father more proud of his son. That day was one of many moments that I would excel on and off the field. Daddy went back to work and proclaimed that I was his champion. Little did he know that he was also mine!

I wished J was well, but she wasn't; arthritis had taken its toll. She fell down and broke her hip and arm at the age of 78. J would never walk again. She had to learn how to adjust to life in a wheelchair. It was hard for her initially. J was a strong independent woman with lots of pride. Depending on someone else wouldn't come easy. Instantly dad's life changed.

We were subservient to her needs, waiting on her night and day! Her condition required an unconditional sacrifice; we had to deny ourselves. It was vital to keep her spirits high and monitor her appetite. J loved seafood and so did I. Sometimes, J called the local fish market and ordered live blue crabs; they were only four dollars a dozen. I walked to the market; it was only a block away. Fortunately, I didn't have to wait long; the crabs were bagged and ready. Patiently, J waited in her wheelchair for my return. She had the water seasoned and ready to go. The tantalizing smell of seafood made our mouths water. Soon, we smeared newspaper across the kitchen table; it was time to eat! J demanded a hammer to crack her crabs with and a can of Budweiser to drink. Sometimes she allowed me to taste it! Daddy didn't like that one bit.

He'd scream, "Momma you know better than to give that boy beer!"

J replied, "Oh Fred, a little beer ain't going to hurt that boy."

I always cracked crabs for her; she would smash too hard with the hammer. However, J ate the crabs faster than I could crack.

She said to me, "Hurry up Joe, you're taking too long!"

Getting my fare share wouldn't come easy, but we always managed to work things out. I treasured every minute we shared.

It was 1978, and I had gotten promoted into the eighth grade. Ribault Jr. was three times the size of Ocean Way, and I was faced with unique challenges. I was very quiet and spent most of my time with Edwin Davis; his friends called him Juke. He was very entertaining and everybody loved him. Most of my friends were beginning to date.

I couldn't believe how most of the girls had developed; they had big breasts and hips. Hormones were on the loose; some became teenage mothers. I had a crush on Shannon Cummings, she was the prettiest girl in school. Most of the pretty girls dated boys in the ninth grade or that played on the football team. I had two problems. I was an eighth grader and didn't play football for the school. I started out with two strikes against me. The guys on the football team were bigger than any player I had ever seen. I weighed only 104 lbs soaking wet! Strike three and I was out! For the first time I had doubts about playing ball. The guys were just too big and strong. The players on the school roster mocked the Pop Warner players; they felt it was for babies. Nevertheless, I continued playing Pop Warner, and I was charmed into playing for the Rattlers. Coach Freddie tried his best to talk me out of leaving the Blazers, but my mind was made up. He even promised to make me the team's MVP.

I asked him, "What if I didn't deserve it? Would you take it from someone that did and give it to me? That wouldn't be the right thing to do." Even back then I stood for what was right. It took a lot of courage to tell him that. I never saw Coach Freddie the same again; his character was assassinated.

The Rattlers had an all-star lineup, and were predicted to win the city championship. Coach Roach was a vocal leader and used tactical shenanigans to improve our performance. His animated approach towards football was comical and intimidating. I thought that he was crazy! Nevertheless, I excelled and scored a 90 yard touchdown on the first day of practice. That was one of many long touchdown runs. The game against my former team stood out more than any other. I felt really bad playing against my former teammates and friends, we had accomplished so much together. The house that I had helped build, I was forced to tear down. We defeated the Blazers and I scored three touchdowns. It was a victory I barely celebrated. We ended with a perfect record. That earned us a chance to play for city champions in the Gator Bowl; it seated 75,000 people! Dad was right there pumping me up. Everybody from his job was there to lend support. Boy, I was nervous! Mr. Moore videotaped the game. We traveled to the Gator Bowl in a Greyhound that night. However, that didn't impress Lakeside at all.

Their squad was big and ferocious, and we considered them a worthy opponent. Despite giving a valiant effort, we suffered our first defeat. We sat on the bench with our hearts ripped out while our opponents were crowned city champs. Dad came onto the field to cheer me up. Losing

never came easy, but he taught me how to bow gracefully in the midst of defeat. Many of my teammates blamed our quarterback for losing the game. I felt his pain. I thought about the passes I dropped with the Blazers that cost us the game. Sympathetically, I embraced him and said, "Get 'em next time!" Chris needed a dad like mine to help him get through a difficult time.

Playing football and maintaining good grades posed a tremendous challenge. Math and history were tough subjects. My English teacher was Ms. Hanna; all the guys had had a crush on her. She tried to help by giving us the answers to the test. At the time I thought that was cool, but I discovered it did more harm than good. It was the first time

I failed the multiple level skills test. Luckily, I got a second chance and that was all I needed.

Meanwhile, Lenny enforced harsh chores around the house. Sometimes, I had to dip half the water out of the pool with a bucket whenever the pump broke. I never complained; I just did it. Mom hated it, but there was nothing she could do.

In less than six months I gained 42 lbs and grew about three inches. This time I was determined to play for my school. Coach Owens was my new coach. He was a big dark skinned man with a beard; he barely cracked a smile. We practiced in the school gym. Slowly, my name became a common topic. My talent surprised many, including myself. It was a boost for my confidence! Sometimes dad came out and watched me practice. I started the season with high expectations; but un-expectantly I was moved to Flanker, an unfamiliar position. I was just an average player and scored only one touchdown. I felt intimidated, thinking that high-school was beyond my ability.

We lost nearly all of our games that year. Nevertheless, that didn't stop me from dreaming about achieving lofty ambitions. I told Coach Owens that I was going to try out for Varsity next year. He told me I wouldn't make it. His words were abrasive and insensitive, but they inspired me to get better. I had to prove him wrong, I couldn't disappoint daddy, he made varsity as a 10th grader and so was I. I started exercising at night. I didn't have weights so I used empty milk jugs filled with sand. To develop my chest muscles I lay against a splintery board and lifted until it burned. That was my first gym! Often, I gazed into the heavens and wondered how far my dreams would take me. I finished my workout with push-ups, dips, and a protein shake before bed. My body transformed overnight into a chiseled hunk of muscle! Daddy always told me that I had to be willing to work harder than all the other running backs. And that's what I did. I made major progress that year.

Dad had a surprise to tell me. It was back to the mountains! This time we brought Emma's grandson Mike with us. Now, I had someone to play with. Mike was about four years younger than me and he was a great running back himself, I became his idol and role model. Like before, we took lots of pictures. Mike and I played every chance we got. One day, we went to the falls and Mike nearly fell in. I grabbed his hand and snatched him up before he slipped. Dad and Emma were impressed over my strength. They were thankful that I saved the day.

Dad was on his way to the top. As a child my dad's image had grown as big as the mountain we visited in Asheville. He could do no wrong. Dad was kind, gentle, funny and smart. I couldn't help but love him. His heart was so big and pure, blinding you to his defeats. He was a good man. We loved spending quality time together. Sometimes, we played basketball at the park. Dad showed signs of his past greatness with pin-point shooting and behind the back dribbles. Whenever I played poorly, he encouraged me to play my best. When dad saw improvement, he shouted these words, "Now you're ready!"

J was extremely proud to see dad's life transformed; it showed in her eyes. Often, she'd sit on the porch and speak to the neighbors. Every day, the mailman would greet her with a friendly smile and shout, "Have a good day Ms. Davis!"

Sitting on the porch with J became a monumental tradition. We discussed everything, from slavery to the second coming of Jesus. My favorite discussions occurred during torrential rainstorms, while lightning danced across the sky. The old folks said it was raining cats and dogs. We turned the lights off and, it was forbidden to speak on the phone; we feared God's wrath. The one thing I loved about my family was that we all trusted and respected each other. Rarely, did I have a problem getting permission to do things or go places because my parents trusted me.

One day, mom took me and a friend to the big rival football game between Ribault and Raines in the Gator Bowl. Most of the urban youth went to see the bands perform. There were plenty of girls in attendance. I had lots of fun that night and I needed to choose which school to attend the following year. I was astounded by their performance; they resembled pros. The running backs were big and fast;

I felt intimidated. Coach Owens appeared to be right, and I questioned my ability to make the varsity team. I had a long, long way to go. That night my heart bled blue and white, and I decided to attend Ribault Senior High. Immediately, I felt the stress of growing up and a dire need to earn a college education. I wanted a scholarship, but I knew I had to get better grades and work harder than ever before. From that moment, my priorities changed. I had a great sense of urgency, but a greater fear of failure.

It started at home. I kept my room clean, my bed was made and my closet was clean. I believed in organization; that was instilled in me at an early age. At night, I ironed my clothes so I didn't have to rush or be late for school. I put my pants under my mattress to keep the crease; a technique I learned from Lenny. That philosophy groomed me into a leader and helped me to deal with adversity on and off the field. I loved the rewards of peace and contentment that came along with being organized and prepared.

The weekend before school started, daddy took me shopping. I attended school to take care of business, so I dressed as a businessman. I was restless the night before, I tossed and turned. There were nearly 3000 students and very few of them knew me. I didn't know what to expect. This was it, high-school; girls and big time football! Many of the players were local legends. I anticipated going on dates, driving to school, and playing high-school football; I couldn't wait!

I was up bright and early the first day. Mom was nervous too, she was up much earlier than usual. She wanted to see me off and wish me well. I was dressed to impress! I walked to school nearly every morning with some of the other kids. I fantasized about having my own car, but I knew that it would all come in due time. The upper classmen proudly pranced around campus; they were reverenced. All the girls hung around the popular seniors.

One day before the end of class, an announcement was made over the intercom. The junior varsity football coach was looking for players. That was music to my ears. After class, I scurried towards the gym to sign up. I was greeted by scores of freshmen just like me. Some of the kids were new and others were not, some were big and others were small. I recognized a couple of guys from the neighborhood and from Pop Warner.

One thing we all hated was running wind sprints. The first day of practice, I ran so much I thought that I was going to die! Coach Furlow, aka Sweet Pea, was a tall, big man that wore an Afro and walked with a limp. He lighted cigars and kept us running until it was all out.

"Down," he said as he blew his whistle. I struggled, but I ran until I had nothing left. Coach had us run for the love of it! Sometimes, we ran with our pads on, other times we ran with them off. The worst thing was running in the heat. Some guys threw up! Others quit and walked away. Coach was only separating the boys from the men. He was pushing us to our limits to determine our level of commitment. Coach wanted to know if we were willing to give our all. Those were valuable lessons that gave me a mental, physical, and spiritual edge in football as well as in life. Slowly, I worked my way to the top of the depth chart, winning a starting position. Daddy was extremely proud.

One Friday I experienced my first pep rally. The cheerleaders enthused the audience and the band played our favorite songs. Kim Brooks seduced me into passion with her impeccable beauty. Somehow, I summoned the courage to ask her out for a date; to my surprise she said yes.

I kept my mind focused on football because the season was about to start. Our first game was against Lake City, a fierce inter-conference rival. It was a competitive game. I rushed for over 100 yards. That was my best performance in two years! It lured the attention of fans, teammates, and Ellis McSwain; the varsity football coach. I heard that he asked lots of questions about me.

After the game Coach Furlow said to me, "That's the way to run that ball boy!" He told daddy that I had no fear.

We finished the regular season undefeated and were rained city champs. McSwain promoted me up to the varsity team to finish the season. That was an honor! The news roamed swiftly, commencing adulation among my peers. I followed daddy's footsteps, I made the varsity team. He was very proud of me. However, my new teammates appeared angry, they snarled and shouted, "We're going to break you in half!"

I was a little concerned. I prayed to God that they wouldn't kill me. I could deal with broken bones; I just didn't want to die! I made it through practice without a scratch. We had only two games left that season. We prepared to play against Tallahassee Lincoln; they ranked 10th in the state of Florida. We left early one Friday morning for Tallahassee. I thought that was cool because we didn't have to go to school. All the players carried their overnight bags and put them on the greyhound bus just before sunrise. Morning dew was on the grass. I felt special as a member of the varsity team. It was exhilarating, and I felt like I was playing in the big leagues. The exposure boosted my confidence in spite of playing an insignificant role. I was the kick returner, something I had never done before. The bus ride was long and tedious. While I slept, my teammates entertained themselves with music.

When we arrived, it was close to game time and we had to quickly get dressed. The football stadium was jammed packed. The band played the school fight song and then there they were. Lincoln High was dressed in red and white. It was time to play football! We received the kick-off. The first time I touched the ball I took it up the middle and back to the outside for 40 yards! My teammates went crazy slapping my helmet and jumping up and down. I couldn't believe that I did it!

With only minutes to play in the game Coach Lee yelled, "Elgin get in there!"

My heart dropped! I made a great run and picked up a first down. That day a legend was born. Lincoln went on to win that game, but we fought hard and I gained the respect of the seniors on my team.

The next week, our season ended with our inner city rival, the Raines Vikings. That week before the game, both schools were trash talking. We hated each other. They even spray painted our school with the word Vikings! Everybody in town was talking about the game. It was a cold frigid Saturday night, with temperatures somewhere in the high 20's! I almost froze to death on the sidelines! I didn't play much, but being on the sidelines with the varsity was gratifying, especially the girls. We lost that game too, and just like that, another season had come and gone.

I didn't play any other sports that year, but I enjoyed going to the basketball games with daddy. The gym was packed, and everyone stared at us as we entered. I looked straight ahead, I was shy. But dad always made time to stop and speak. That was the kind of dad I had; a heart as big as Texas with a sense of humor to match!

One day dad and I went car shopping. We pulled up next to the hottest car on the lot; dad got out for a closer look. It was a two tone gray Riviera! It was nice, real nice. The salesperson came to greet us. He threw dad the keys to crank it up and look inside. It had leather and all kinds of fancy displays, more than I had ever seen!

I told dad that I wished the car was ours. "We could drive it anywhere, even to the White House!" I started to feel bad because it wasn't ours.

Dad smiled. He threw me the keys and said, "Son it's ours!"

I couldn't believe it. Dad had already bought it, he wanted to surprise me! I jumped as high as I could over and over again. That was one of the happiest days of my life! We drove around town showing our friends the new car. Daddy was evolving; he was on his way to the top. He was a perfect example for those that struggled with adversity. The Lord was working through him. Daddy taught me to love God and to trust in him no matter how bad things got; I loved him for that. Dad became a perfect example for me too!

At home things were disastrous; mom and Lenny argued relentlessly. Sometimes, I heard them late at night. It made me very upset because mom cried a lot.

I would say, "Momma, stop crying."

She told me that she'd be alright. My dislike for Lenny intensified. Sometimes days would go by without a word being spoken in the house. I felt the tension and stress.

After one argument, mom said, "I hope you (Lenny) die and never come back!"

She was hurting bad, real bad, and so was I. I was supportive and tried to do nice things for momma. I found strength and an inner peace when I prayed. I grew up as a praying child, especially when things got bad.

One day, mom went to Georgia. When she returned, Lenny had the whole yard plowed. He grew a garden in the front yard, we were shocked. Mom and I were embarrassed, it was a mess. Spectators slowed down in their cars and stared. We were the laughing stock of the neighborhood.

My friends snickered, and asked, "Why ya'll did that to your yard?"

I was at a loss for words.

Lenny valued the opinions of the 700 Club. He was convinced we needed to grow our own food to ensure survival. We had no influence in the decision at all; we were prisoners in our own home.

What I learned in church and football helped me to accept things I didn't understand. Prayer helped me the most. Mom never stayed unhappy for long; she had too much joy inside of her. I learned how to find peace and joy in any situation from her example. That's how I defeated my enemies and overcame obstacles.

To escape from pain, I spent my free time with dad and J doing fun stuff. One of the funniest times I had was going fishing at Ortega Park. Dad baited the area with fish food, schools of fish surfaced to eat it! There were people lined up all along the bank fishing for mullet. An elderly lady sat near daddy on a bucket while he was throwing out fish grain. When we looked down, the ladies head was filled with fish food! We laughed so hard and nobody knew why. Dad was too embarrassed to say a word. Suddenly, she caught a fish and fell backwards right on her face! The fish flapped in her face and when she stood up, sand covered her face. Everybody tried not to laugh, it was impossible not to; dad and I fell out! Dad's fishing skills weren't much better. That day dad snatched the fish so hard, all that came back on his hook was the fishes' lips! Now you talk about funny; that was funny! At day's end, we caught multitudes of mullet. It was days like that that made growing up as a child so special.

Later, we took a family trip to Lakeland, Georgia. J cooked lots of food for the trip. It was a southern tradition to take food when staying over night. J said it showed respect and kept people from talking about you when you left. I guess they really respected us because J must have taken enough food to last a year! I knew that dad didn't mind because he loved eating. Quickly we hit the road, and as usual dad had all of his old music.

J complained about the music being too loud; she'd rather have silence. She was unwilling to compromise. They both were stubborn and argued for most of the trip. We couldn't please J.

She kept shouting, "Fred slow down, Fred the music is too loud!"

It was Fred this and Fred that! She even tried to tell dad how to drive, although she had never driven before! Dad finally had had enough of J's smart mouth and did the unthinkable. He stopped the car on the side of the highway and put his mother out of the car, wheelchair and all. I couldn't believe it! Daddy sped off. I could see J out of the back window just sitting there.

I said, "Dad we can't leave J!" After driving only a block he backed up the car and picked her up. Of course was only joking, but J didn't think it was funny.

When she got back in the car she said these words in a smart tone, "You didn't have to come back you know! I got plenty of money!" J didn't take shit from anybody, including dad. Remarkably they stopped arguing.

In Lakeland we talked about old times and ate wild game; that was right up J's alley. When it came time for bed, dad and I slept on the patio. The mosquitoes ate us alive! We couldn't take it anymore so we slept in the car with the air conditioning running. Nevertheless, we had a nice time and it did us good to get away.

When we got home, it was time for the fair. Very few events integrated our community, but the Jacksonville Agricultural Fair did just that. Succulent aromas and sounds of roaring roller coasters attracted families beyond racial, social, and political barriers. Mom and I were the first in line. After buying tickets, we had just enough money to buy a candy apple; they were moms favorite. Cooler temperatures were a rare treat. We bundled up tightly and paraded under the starry nights of autumn. A myriad of food, fun, and entertainment capsulated the moment. Mom's joyful spirit helped me to treasure being a kid.

I developed a deeper appreciation for life and I enjoyed helping others; it was my way of giving charity. Humility became my greatest attribute, and it gained God's favor more than any other quality. The spirit of sharing made my heart grow; it was medicine for the soul. The more I gave, the more I received.

I was greatly admired and given wonderful compliments. Many said that I was special and would be a great man someday I smiled and said, "Thank you." My school teachers had me stand up in the front of the class and complimented my character. I was flattered to say the least, but it was a lot of pressure to live up to.

One day, Ms. Vaun, my history teacher, told me to go next door and just tell the teacher my name.

I did. The teacher stood up, shook my hand and said "It's a pleasure to meet you."

Observers noticed something about me other than football; that was a great feeling. Sometimes daddy rewarded me with the keys to the Riviera. I went on several dates, but the conversation never drifted far away from football; it perpetually consumed me. I studied all the great running backs to emulate as many moves and techniques as possible. I wanted to be the best running back ever! They were lofty ambitions but I was determined. Daddy always taught me to aim high.

I admired Herschel Walker, the greatest college running back I'd ever seen. He was 6'1", 225 lbs with world class speed. He became the yardstick in which I measured myself. I was only 5'9" and 165 lbs. I was a child compared to him, and it would take a miracle. I started working out in the weight room after school. I asked our best player for help. Anthony Quiller was a beast, and his presence was intimidating, but he was as gentle as a lamb. He worked me mercilessly. Dizzy and nauseated, I'd vomit to relieve myself. But he showed no sympathy; he pushed me like a drill sergeant. The results were astonishing! Soon, I resembled a well defined athlete.

High school wouldn't have been the same without Jack Johnson. I loved him with all my heart. He was the brother that I never had, and our intrinsic values made us a good influence on each other. Nothing was beyond his ability; Jack was a man among boys! He taught me how to drive a stick shift. One day while driving home from school, he pulled over his Chevy Nova and insisted I take the wheel. I looked at him like he was insane, but he told me I could do it. The car skipped and stalled all the way home! Thanks to Jack, I made it.

We enjoyed going to the movies, hanging out, and listening to our favorite band, Zap. There was one song in particular, <u>More Bounce</u>

<u>to the Once</u>. We became very popular around school. Jack and I were like two peas in a pod.

It was close to Christmas break, and I couldn't wait to go to Jesup. That trip changed my life; I met a special girl.

Valerie Fuqua was my soul mate, she melted my heart. I met Val at my grandparents' house while she was running errands. She gave me the warmest smile and had a gap between her teeth as big as the state of Texas; I thought it was so cute. We established instant rapport and could've talked for hours. I hated to see her leave. However, she returned. I was infatuated by her impeccable charm, and she ensured me that the feelings were mutual. Val unexpectedly jolted me with disturbing news, she had a boyfriend. My world came to a screeching halt. I tried to act tough but couldn't. My vital signs were weakening because I felt like dying. Val reached into her purse and gave me a tape to listen to; it was love songs. That's the night I fell in love.

Christmas break was over and I returned home with a broken heart. Focusing on school and athletics was challenging, but my future depended on it! 1980 was a great year for our football program. Five players received scholarships to Division II colleges to play football. I was thrilled. It showed me the rewards of hard work and dedication. However, I wanted more. I wanted bigger and I wanted better. I wanted Division I football, the best. That would take lots of work and a little luck. I was willing and able. When spring practice started I was #3 on the depth chart, but I knew that deep inside I was better and I was going to prove it. I never worked harder at anything before in all my life. I worked out in the heat of the day to stay in peak condition. I didn't regret paying a price to become the best. Daddy insisted that I stay out of the sun; I was turning dark, very dark. My peers began making jokes about my complexion. They used mean spirited words such as blacky and tar baby to describe me. My feelings were bruised and I felt unattractive. Over the next three years I used creams to bleach my skin before going to bed. The lighter my skin became the better I felt about myself. I wish making the starting lineup was as easy as bleaching my skin. I didn't play one down in our spring jamboree game. I heard the college football scouts attended that game, but none of them saw me play that night.

The good news was I had gotten promoted into the 11th grade. I always looked for the positive things in life. Getting older required such wisdom and responsibility. My choices were crucial to my survival. An error could have been detrimental, if not fatal; especially within the black community. Many of my friends had gotten into trouble with the law and became a statistic. Some experimented with reefer, smoking cigarettes, and drinking alcohol. Others became teenage fathers! Dad told me if I hung around with nine bad guys I'd be the tenth. I chose the right path. I wasn't perfect; Jack and I enjoyed drinking beer. Schlitz's Malt Liquor Bull was our favorite. One or two sips was all it took for me and Jack to feel good. Jack's new car was a blue Grand Prix; he installed 12 inch sub woofers. We based out, you could hear us from blocks away! Sometimes Ed, Vernon, and Tyrus would accompany us. They were our friends.

One night we double dated. Jack drove to the school and parked in the back to smooch. Jack sat up front and I sat in the rear. Suddenly, a loud noise erupted. Security had locked the gate and driven away! The outcome wasn't favorable, it warranted a suspension from school; we had to escape. Jack surprised everybody when he jumped out of the car and walked to the front of the gate. Someone shouted, "What is he doing?"

Suddenly, he grabbed the gate and shook it uncontrollably until it broke off the hinges. We were in shock. I mumbled, "Damn, did you see that!"

Jack returned to the car out of breath; nobody said a word.

Also, we lounged around the mall. The Gateway was a black mall enriched with cultural tradition. Fancy paint jobs on pimped out cars attracted throngs; celebrated personalities occasionally attended. Gateway became a bench mark of pride.

The richest and most glorifying tradition among the black community occurred on Sunday mornings. The church was our solution of coping with our pain and oppression. Reverend Dailey was a dynamic preacher. Often, he'd acknowledge my presence. He told me that I was a fine young man, and said a special prayer for me.

Some weekends dad and I would feast like kings; barbeque ribs were our favorite. He'd start eating the ribs on one end and I'd start on the other, but I always reached the middle first.

Dad said, "Hey man, you're on my side."

But he always allowed me to continue. He was a free hearted man that enjoyed seeing others happy. J's condition was weakening; she required more attention. She was unable to use the restroom on her own; sometimes she'd urinate or defecate on herself. Daddy dreaded bathing her, the slightest touch erupted howls that could be heard across the room. It was hard to bare, sometimes I vacated the home. She had always been strong and independent. Now, she was as helpless as a child. The most beautiful thing was watching dad's love and tenderness. Sometimes, I'd watch him feed J. He was gentle and caring, yet so strong and powerful. I gained a greater respect for my daddy; he sacrificed his life for her. Dad had no brothers or sisters to help.

J called out day and night, "Fred, hey Fred!"

Dad said, "Yes momma?"

I helped him with many of the responsibilities; it was too much for one person. J's condition troubled her; she didn't want to be a burden. She began drinking Gin. At her age, drinking wasn't good, it only made things worse. Sometimes I hid the bottle, but J had somebody in the neighborhood buy her more. Caring for her was almost impossible.

They got into big arguments. Dad was only trying to help. J didn't want anybody telling her what to do, she was stubborn.

J's condition required constant care. He loathed the idea of leaving J home alone. However, he had no choice, he earned minimal wages and the cost of living became demanding. But God made us rich where it counted the most!

I hated to leave dad and J struggling and return home to a comfortable lifestyle; I grieved. Lenny made sure I had enough work to occupy my mind. One day, Lenny unloaded a pile of heavy wooden beams in the driveway. He demanded me to relocate them; I struggled for hours. Mom pleaded, "Why are you working that boy like that?"

Lenny replied, "You stay out of it!"

Reasoning with him was difficult. He dominated the conversation when you'd voice your opinion. For the sake of peace I remained silent; he became enraged. He threw a brick in my vicinity, I erupted! Lenny told me to get out of his house. It happened so fast I didn't have time to put on my clothes; I ran down across the street practically naked. Friends saw me running; they knew something was terribly wrong. I must have run about two miles before mom picked me up. Nervously, I sat in the back seat hyperventilating. Gradually, mom's soothing words consoled me and my breathing was restored to normal.

Football was my fortress, and I looked forward to the upcoming season; it gave me a new outlook on life. With two losing seasons it was time for a new coach. Don Gaffney, a young charismatic leader answered the call; he knew all the right words to say to rebuild our confidence. His glamorous popularity induced excitement. I couldn't have asked for a better opportunity. My ship had finally come in.

Coach Gaffney called me Baby Herschel; he said I ran just like him. I loved hearing that. He told me that if I wanted to be a great back, I needed to get faster and the only way was to run track. I hated track, too much running. But he convinced me and Jack to join the track team. Coach Gaffney said he wanted to always see me and Jack together; that was fine with us, we loved being together. Coach Helm was our coach, a man I love to this day. He contributed much to my success. Track turned out to be a blessing in disguise. We had three All-Americans on the team that year and we led the nation with the fastest time in the 440 relay. I struggled, and so did Jack. He was too big and clumsy; he was better equipped for throwing the disk or shot put. Eventually, Jack quit the team, he gave it his best but it wasn't good enough. With perseverance and dedication I blossomed into a contender; I loved track.

Running track helped me to become a better football player; Coach Gaffney was right. I ran at an accelerated pace. I learned how to regulate my breathing; that proved to be a great advantage on the football field. Soon, track was over and it was time for spring football.

I had to have a stellar year, there was no tomorrow. I was committed more than ever, and was willing to pay the price. During our first practice I suffered a concussion. A defender viciously tackled me from behind. My head ricochet off the surface and dismantled my memory. I didn't know my name. I went home and fell asleep, and didn't tell a soul; not even mom.

Some nights before bed, I practiced plays in the middle of the road. Other nights, I did push-ups until my arms were swollen. After working out I swam laps in the pool. When I was done, I laid down; I was exhausted. I changed my diet; I stopped eating at McDonalds and Burger King. I loved double cheeseburgers. However, I loved football more. I even stopped drinking soda! I drank water and juice. I was in peak condition, 185 lbs of muscle. I was strong, fast, dedicated, and determined! I was ready to play football!

I often reminisced of Val, I wanted to see her. Momma permitted me to call long distance; Val was ecstatic to hear my voice. We talked for hours. She told me that she had broken up with her boyfriend. I must have jumped ten feet in the air! I didn't waste any time asking her to be my girl; she said yes.

It was summer and I made plans to visit Val. Daddy had reservations. He saw disturbing signs and preferred me to stay. I was passionate about my desire and promised to act responsible.

When I arrived in Georgia, Val greeted me at the bus station. She was vivacious and fulfilled all of my expectations. We had so much fun. Some nights we gazed into the heavens wishing upon a star. Other times we took drives along the countryside. I was completely committed and vowed to always treat her right.

The summer had quickly evaporated and I abandoned town. However, I left a piece of my heart in Georgia; I was depressed. I couldn't suppress my feelings; I loved her.

It was my final year of high school. There were many special moments, but none greater than when Auntie bought me a car. It was a blue Pinto with a missing hubcap. It wasn't the prettiest car, but I was grateful that I didn't have to walk to school. I put a big house speaker in the back window and listened to Third World; I loved reggae.

I was recognized as the top dog on campus. I had stepped into the shoes of those mentors that preceded me. I was happy to see my teammates; especially Jack. It was time to play football; we showcased a heroic squad. Two of my teammates were exceptional. Kelvin Martin was an accomplished receiver. Daddy called him "silk" because he was so smooth! Kelvin ended a great NFL career culminating with two

Super Bowl victories with the Dallas Cowboys. Naz Worthen could catch a B.B. in the dark! He was drafted by the Kansas City Chiefs. We had undeniable talent, and set our focus on a state title.

In my senior year book, I quoted playing professional football as my life long ambition. I was embarrassed because most students chose respectful careers such as doctors and lawyers. Nevertheless, I swallowed my pride and worked toward accomplishing my dream; destiny was on my side. Back then, football was fun and innocent. We played for the love of it! We'd buckle up our chin straps and play ball. I plunged intellectually and discovered that politics influenced the game. Many players were denied the opportunity to play. Hate festered in my heart toward the game that I dedicated my life.

The lessons that I learned from Lenny were beginning to make sense, and I discovered that Lenny wasn't a bad man; he was brilliant! I thank God for helping me to evolve spiritually, and denounce bitterness and hatred. I found forgiveness in my heart for the years of bad memories that I held Lenny responsible for. And for the first time, I felt a special bond with him. He was the smartest and wisest man I had ever known, and I realized that he loved me!

Meanwhile, Coach Gaffney took football to another level, practice started at 5AM; it was pitch black outside. I had to delve deep within and motivate myself to continue. The weak minded complained, but

I never said a word. Practice was never easy. I had to learn how to overcome pain, frustration and difficult situations. It took everything I had, but I learned how to condition my mind. That rare attribute made me an instant leader. I was captain of the football team, an honor that I treasure even to this day. I tried my best to live up to high expectations! It was time to play football.

Our first game was against Sandalwood High School. I ran like a horse; I was fatigued. I rushed over a hundred yards but that wasn't good enough; we lost by one point. We were disappointed, but I realized that losing was a part of winning, and I focused on our next opponent.

That next morning, momma came running into my room hollering, "Elgin wake up, wake up! You're in the newspaper!"

Unexpectedly, I made the front page of the Jacksonville Times Union. My family was very proud, and so was I. The next week, a news reporter came to interview me. I didn't know what to expect; it was my first time conducting an interview. It was a huge article with a big picture of me on the front page. I received letters from many of the top colleges in the south; Florida, Florida State, Richmond, Florida A & M, Bethune Cookman, Central Florida, Miami, Kentucky, Oklahoma State, Mississippi State and Tulane. Who's Who in America acknowledged my accomplishments; I was loving it! I was voted president of The Fellowship of Christian Athletes. My skills blossomed.

I benched 350lbs and ran a 4.4 forty. From that day on I was known as the Trojan Horse.

My 946 yards gained me all-conference honors and lured college scouts. We finished 6-5 that year, a disappointing season with so much talent. At one point, we were ranked as the number 10 team in the state of Florida, however we quickly plummeted. Scouts from Florida A & M and Bethune Cookman came to visit me, but I made myself unavailable; I didn't want to attend a small school. Those tactics nearly shattered my dream of playing college football. The major colleges reneged on their previous offers. I was baffled and my heart was broken. Later it was alleged that Coach Gaffney blocked the schools from seeing me, he wanted Jack and I to go as a package. Kelvin experienced similar problems. Despite being the city's most prolific receiver, he had to campaign his own way to Boston College. Something was awry, especially when players in our same district signed scholarships to attend major colleges.

SECTION II: NOON

Well, we couldn't wait for coach anymore. We had to do something fast, because time was running out. Then the most beautiful thing happened. My family came together for the first time and got busy. Lenny and Auntie started making calls to different schools and dad worked on gathering and sending out game films. Mom got busy praying. I felt very special. Auntie drew first blood. She and her friend Heyward called Valdosta State and set up a meeting with the coach. I was very nervous; I had never been on a college campus. Valdosta was a small school, just a little bigger than Ribault. It was rich in football tradition. However, Valdosta wasn't for me.

Suddenly, Lenny had an idea. He picked up the phone and called the University of Georgia athletic department; Vince Dooley answered. Lenny was the perfect representative. I don't know what he said but Coach Dooley wanted me at Georgia. I was ecstatic. However, there was a dilemma. Georgia had expended their scholarships. My only choice was to try out as a walk on. Coach Dooley promised that if I was good enough, he'd offer me a scholarship later. My pride was wounded and I felt like a failure; I wanted a scholarship. That was my goal since a little boy; my hopes were bleak. But, there was no time to feel sorry for myself. I had to straighten up fast, there were major concerns we had to overcome; like paying college tuition. We didn't have any money, but mom and Lenny told me not to worry. I realized how much my family loved me; I was deeply touched. We applied for financial aid. Daddy filled out the forms and prepared to send them out. I was thrilled about attending the University of Georgia to play football. The Bulldogs were the NCAA champions. Everyone was relieved. Suddenly, I received a phone call. Auntie had spoken with a scout from the University of Central Florida that expressed an interest in me. Jeremiah Davis was invited to our house for dinner. We were all impressed; his character was sublime. He was excited about their new football program and head coach. Lou Saban was a fierce competitor; he hated losing with a passion. He was the head coach for the Buffalo Bills when O.J. Simpson set an NFL rushing record of 2000 yards in a single season. Coach Davis told me that if I wanted to play in the NFL, Coach Saban could help. He told me that if I went to UCF I could play my freshman year. Plus, the campus was close to home. It all made sense, but UCF was a Division II football team. That meant no big crowds or national television exposure.

I had mixed feelings until Mr. Davis told me there was one scholarship left and it was mine if I wanted it. That was great news to my family and I; it relieved a multitude of burdens. I had two days to give Coach Davis an answer. I went back to the basics and I dropped to my knees and asked God to help me. And he did.

Dad said to me, "Son, I'd rather be a big fish in a little pond, than a little fish in a big pond."

The choice was simple; I was going to the University of Central Florida. Thank you daddy for being there for me when I needed you most. Thank you Lenny for your support and effort. Thank you Auntie, without you it wouldn't have been possible, and thank you momma for keeping it all together and for your unconditional love! Thanks ya'll! We made it! We made it! Thank God we made it!

Early one Saturday morning, we drove to the University of Central Florida. Mom and dad talked to me about life. They told me that they were proud of me and to continue serving God. I never said a word. Soon, we were in Orlando. Dad was pretty good with directions, and we found the campus without any problems. I felt butterflies as we drove into campus. Everyone was nervous; especially dad.

We met with Coach Davis at the athletic building. He explained the agenda before escorting us around campus. I was very nervous, and I made sure not to drift far from his side. Our first stop was the training room. It was equipped with fancy machines and state of the art whirlpools; it looked intimidating. He observed my reactions, and asked, "You alright big man?"

I assured him with a nod. Coach Davis was just what I needed; a father figure away from home. While touring the campus, Coach Davis suggested we take a picture. We concurred, and the seven of us gathered together and took a beautiful photo. The picture brings a smile and warmth to my heart even to this day. At that time, UCF only had about 14,000 students enrolled, but from my eyes it looked like a little city.

Coach Davis said I was going to love Orlando, and he also had something special to show me. We all jumped in the van and took a short trip into town. Orlando was a beautiful city with lots of attractions. The interstate highway was clustered with tourists heading to Disney World. I reminisced about our vacation when I was a little boy. Coach showed me our home field; The Citrus Bowl. It was huge! I visualized myself running down the sideline scoring the winning touchdown. Back then, it was only a dream, but later it became a reality.

On the way back to the campus, Lenny asked lots of good questions. Coach Davis had lots of good answers. There was only one thing left to do; meet Coach Saban and sign my scholarship.

As we approached his office, my voice trembled and my heart raced. Suddenly, the room appeared dark and I struggled to maintain my balance. Desperately, I made my way to the water fountain for a cool drink. Finally, the moment I had been waiting for had arrived. With a lump nestled in my throat, sweat on my brow, and tears in my eyes, I met the legendary Lou Saban.

My family was well pleased; it was a monumental moment. Coach Saban greeted me with a stern smile. He was a distinguished, middle aged man with gray hair. It was obvious that he was a strong negotiator. We shook hands and discussed his expectations for student athletes. After I agreed to the rules, he offered me a four year scholarship. Nervously, I signed my name on the dotted line and became an official UCF Knight. That's when mom and Auntie started crying; they were exceedingly joyful.

On the way back to Jacksonville, we stopped at Red Lobster to celebrate my success. It was the first time that we had gathered for such an occasion.

The following week, my success had made headlines; I was featured in the local newspaper. I felt like a celebrity, especially when my teammates mobbed me at school. Like those before me, my name was mentioned over the intercom; it was a great feeling. Finally, my hard work and dedication had paid off, and God's grace and mercy prevailed. Most of my teammate's athletic careers came to a finale; like Jack Johnson. I felt so badly for him, he should have gotten a scholarship; it just wasn't fair.

That Sunday in church, Reverend Dailey announced that I received a scholarship. He gave me my first Bible. I cherished my Bible and became acquainted with many verses throughout the difficult and trying years.

The congregation showered me with love. Joe and Hazel Reed, a devoted couple, ensured me of their prayers. They told dad I was going to make it; a smile emerged on his face. Mr. Reed informed me that his daughter was attending UCF. I was anxious to meet her, and puzzled why I'd never seen her. Renita was flattering; I was happy to make her acquaintance.

We headed home for dinner and to inform J about the good news. J's approval was unorthodox; however, no one was as proud. J had started a college fund for me when I was a little baby. However, the Afro Life Insurance Company went out of business and I never saw a dime of that money. We accomplished a lot that week. But the real challenge was just ahead. It was time to refocus and finish my senior year strong. Coach said that I could jeopardize losing my scholarship if my grades dropped below a 2.0 GPA. With only a 2.3, I had to buckle down; I had too much to lose.

I finished the track season with all-state honors. We had two major meets, The Bob Hayes and The Trojan Invitational. The Bob Hayes was the nation's largest high school meet; the competition was steep! Bob Hayes took a special interest in me; he and dad went to school together. He was a great inspiration. Bob won two gold medals in the 1964 Olympics in Tokyo. He also played with the Dallas Cowboys and was nicknamed "Bullet Bob." He literally altered the defensive game because of his blazing speed.

Later that week, Keith Stallings signed with Elon College, Reggie Northrup with Cheney State, and Kelvin Martin with Boston College. Jack enrolled into a vocational school in Tampa. Jack and I were less than 70 miles from each other; a dream come true.

On senior skip day, Jack and I went to the beach; I smoked my first joint. It was called a roach, because it had only two or three puffs left. I ended up choking and burning my lips. The more I coughed, the more Jack laughed. That was the last time I smoked weed; it wasn't for me.

I won athlete of the year. That was a great honor, especially when I remembered the legendary winners of the past. Who would've believed that I would have been honored with such a great legacy? God is good, what he did for others, he did for me.

It was time to graduate from high school. This was the moment I had been waiting for. I reminisced about the early years. The trials and tribulations, the pain and bitterness, the laughter and tears; through it all I remained grateful. I wept for those that fell short along the way; the hearts that were broken and never healed, and the dreams that were

shattered. I survived, thank God I survived. I took a picture with dad and Emma at the graduation. There was something special about that picture. Maybe it was dad's big smile!

However, good fortune had eluded Val; her application to attend UCF was denied. I felt bad, but I had to keep moving forward.

The anxiety of going to college was frightening, and I was beginning to feel home sick. Many nights I lay in bed and stared at the ceiling. Throughout the summer, I listened to lots of music and meditated. One day, I challenged myself not to listen to any familiar radio stations. I wanted to grow culturally and learn about different music. It was challenging, but I started learning the names and songs of different artists. I enjoyed bands like U2, The Police, Human Legends, Men at Work, and John Cougar. I made another great accomplishment. My favorite song was <u>Hurt so Good</u> by John Cougar. I love it to this day!

Preparing for college was more difficult than we imagined; there was so much stuff to pack. I felt like leaving it all behind. Mom bought me a blue trunk to put my things in. Each week she purchased items I needed; she didn't want to wait until the last minute. Mom was wise.

In between packing and working out, I made one last stop in Georgia to say goodbye. I had no idea when I would see Val again, but I promised to write every week and call as much as possible. However, saying good-bye to J was much harder; her health was declining. She really needed me, but I was going away. I felt guilty; I didn't want to abandon her. She gave me a foundation and taught me ecumenical principles. For years, it was only the three of us; we were all that we had. It was up to me to keep the family legacy alive. Somehow, deep in my heart, I knew J wouldn't want it any other way. Going forward and reaching my destiny, would keep the name and legacy alive in her honor. I took my challenge very seriously, the people I loved depended on me; I refused to let them down.

I had one night to preserve memories that would last a life time. I stared at the back of my door that read, <u>Chicago Bears Here I Come</u>

and wept. I thanked God for the love that my parents demonstrated to me. Thank you momma, daddy, Lenny, J, Auntie, and Emma! That night, I felt comfort and inner peace within my soul. I had been given a good foundation, and with God's help I could move mountains. My fears subsided, and I knew that God would grant me victory. I was only hours away from entering college.

With all our planning, we found ourselves rushing to make it into Orlando before noon; we were moving like ants. Mom and Lenny argued over petty things. Finally, we got the station wagon loaded. Stacy, mom, Lenny, and I left in one car. Dad, Emma, and Auntie followed in another. Lenny accelerated to speeds beyond 100 mph.

Mom was afraid, she yelled, "Lenny, you need to slow this car down!" Sometimes he did, and sometimes he didn't.

Once we arrived on campus my family hung around while I was assigned my dorm room. After checking in, the players met in the cafeteria annex. I was very nervous, some of the guys were mammoth! I was among fifty-two other freshmen that reported to camp. The freshmen appeared to be sizing each other up and bragging about their high school careers. High school was irrelevant; college was on a totally different level. I ate lunch and met with my family one last time. It got a little mushy. Mom and Auntie were always emotional and this time was no different.

Lenny said, "Come on ya'll. It's time for El to do his thing. We need to go now and leave him alone."

It was difficult for him, but he was only trying to be strong and keep the family together. I walked them to the car and hugged each family member. I assured them that I was going to be alright. Somehow I knew that they received that confirmation; that made leaving a little easier. I watched the car pull away. Mom and Stacy turned around and stared out the rear window and waved goodbye. Then, they were gone.

Polk Hall room 121-B became my home away from home. I sat on the edge of my bed and stared for hours before unpacking. I decided to take a walk around campus. That's when I met a charismatic freshman with a big jerry curl. Teddy Wilson and I hit it off right away. Teddy and I set records at UCF that many athletes would read about and strive to perfect. Those honors earned us our place in history as the first two players drafted into the NFL.

UCF was miles away from town. There wasn't much to do around campus. Teddy had a gold Camaro. We drove miles into town getting familiar with Orlando. Soon, our escapade came to an abrupt end. We had to return to campus and attend team meetings. The staff went over the rules, classes, and answered any questions we had. I was very lonely because I didn't have a roommate. I sat in my room and listened to music.

Registering for classes was easy because the athletes had first pick. I enrolled in many advanced classes.

After registration we had a team meeting. Our most celebrated player was an electrifying runner from Kissimmee, FL. Lorenzo "Chicken" Rivers rushed for over 1900 yards in high school and was deemed as UCF's savior. The media surrounded him like the paparazzi. That motivated me to be the best. No one believed in me as much as Coach Davis.

The night before practice I made sure to get plenty of sleep and say my prayers. I was awaken around 5:30 and met with Coach Pete, the running back coach. He was a mild mannered man with an effervescent spirit; I loved him. Wearing baby blue shoes, I stood out among my teammates. The guys mocked me saying, "Don't step on his blue suede shoes!" I just cracked a smile.

The temperatures in Orlando were smoldering; practice was intolerable. I was featured as the team's third string running back; I saw limited action. I waited patiently before getting an opportunity to practice. On my first carry, I ripped through the defense and gained 25 yards. I emerged from the pile as a legend.

I noticed Chicken and the other backs looking at me strangely; I had gained their respect, and they feared the inevitable.

After practice Ted came over and said, "You looked good man. The coaches were talking about you!"

That made me feel real good but there was no time for talking because we had meetings and a second practice to attend. That left very little time for socializing. We practiced so much I lost count with the days of the week. It was football in the morning, evening, and night. I was sore from the top of my head to the bottom of my feet. I drank lots of water and got plenty of sleep. I was too tired for anything else. I felt like a Hebrew slave during the time of Pharos in Egypt. It was starting to take its toll on me. I lost eight pounds the first day of practice. Coach Pete asked me if I was feeling okay. He told me to go to the cafeteria and eat, so I did. I never had a problem being obedient. That principle gained me respect and blessings throughout my life.

The next practice ushered in a cycle of injuries that eventually ended my football career. During practice, I attempted to navigate through a congested defensive line when Darryl Rudd tumbled awkwardly onto my ankle. The pain was excruciating; I feared that my ankle was broken.

I shouted, "Get up, get up, my ankle my ankle!" I couldn't move.

Darryl asked, "You alright?"

All the trainers trotted towards me yelling, "Don't move, don't move!"

With their shoulders under my arms, they helped me off the field.

Coach Saban said in his legendary voice, "You alright kid?"

I replied, "Yes sir."

My ankle inflated into the size of a grapefruit! It looked awful, but it wasn't broken. I was given a pair of crutches and a strong dose of pain medication. Treatment included submerging my ankle into a bucket of iced water. It took weeks to get used to that but I did. I hated to call home with bad news; I didn't want them to worry about me. Dad insisted on driving down. I assured him that I was fine, but he was determined on coming.

Throughout the week I attended meetings and watched practice from the sidelines; I felt worthless. After a couple of days of treatment, I showed improvement and didn't need crutches anymore. One Saturday morning, daddy unexpectedly arrived; I was ecstatic! His presence initiated a healing. Daddy met with the coaches and discussed my well being.

He returned, shook my hand and said, "Son, I just want to tell you how proud I am of you. You wouldn't believe what the coaches said about you."

I never asked him what they said. I just replied, "Thank you."

Coach Saban insisted I spend the day with my family.

We assembled to Ronnie and Miller's house. It was refreshing leaving campus, I forgot that there was life besides football. Time quickly fled, and dad had to rush back to Jacksonville to attend to J. I was saddened to see him leave. I loved my daddy, and there wasn't a father anywhere that loved their son more than he loved me.

I returned to my room and discovered a stranger was sitting inside. He was Kenny Wright, my new roommate. He was an academic All-American. Kenny took the word "study" to another level. He studied endlessly. Tension mounted, as restrictions were imposed. Talks on the phone or listening to the radio easily distracted him. Sometimes, I got angry when he asked me to turn it down, or when he gave me one of those looks. But, I respected his passion for school; he never had to tell me twice. Kenny had aspirations of playing Major League Baseball and graduating with a degree in marketing. God gave me the perfect roommate; he exemplified the epitome of dedication and perseverance.

The arrival of the general student population ushered excitement around campus, and it was very easy to become distracted. The football team had a mandatory study hall; no exceptions! I spent most of that time writing Val letters; I really missed her. She wrote back two or three times a week. Val had been accepted to Savannah State in Georgia.

Football was cheerful; we had ended two-a-days. We played our first game against Elizabeth City College. Coach Saban was reluctant to dress me; he felt my ankle needed more rest. However, the energy in the stadium was captivating; we drew a feisty crowd. Terrance Bonner led our team to victory, and was voted the most valuable player.

The next week I received good news. I was projected to play in my first college game against the Georgia Southern Eagles. I chose #44. Cautiously, the trainers wrapped my ankles in a special brace; it provided extra support. Before arriving in Statesboro, Coach Pete informed me that I was starting at running back. I was astounded; but it was my destiny. We had an atrocious start, and made foolish mistakes that hindered our progress. The home-field crowd applauded as we crumbled apart. Minutes before half time our luck changed, and we were inches away from Georgia Southern's goal line. Suddenly, I was asked to go in and score a touchdown. It was a perfect hand off, but before crossing the goal line I was plastered by two defenders. The football was dislodged and Georgia Southern recovered it. I blew it! I trotted off the field and sat on the bench with my head down. My teammates tried to encourage me, but I felt horrible.

Suddenly, I heard a voice in the crowd screaming, "That's alright son! Get'em next time!"

It was my daddy; I recognized his voice. Quickly, I turned and waved. We entered half time tied 0-0. That's when Coach Red scared the living daylight out of me. He used curse words that I didn't know existed! In his rage, he threw his clipboard at me. My pride was wounded and I was determined to atone for my mistake. I pleaded for a second chance. We returned to the field with a determined game plan. I carried the ball thirty-one times; a new school record! Then, it happened on a play called 92 draw; I scored a 52 yard touchdown! I compiled a 136 yards, also a record. I had redeemed myself by leading my team to victory. My performance lured a multitude of media; I was a star!

Dad was extremely proud. Later, we ate dinner with the team at a nearby restaurant I was exhausted and dizzy from a vicious blow on the head; I never told a soul though, not even dad. He brought me a stalk of sugar cane to take back to school. But I couldn't wait; I ripped into it like a wild man! The guys thought I was nuts. As dad prepared to drive home, he yawned and rubbed his eyes. I worried about his safety because he was exhausted, and hours away from home.

I was on a roll because the next game I rushed over 100 yards against Southeast Louisiana. My success nurtured envy among my rivals, but I remained humble. Teddy also contributed to our victory by returning a kickoff for a touchdown. After the game I walked on Bourbon Street; I had a blast. I thought about mom and dad a lot; I wanted to share my joy. Football exposed me to opportunities that my parents couldn't fathom. It didn't seem fair. However, I called and shared my experiences with them.

Meanwhile, Chicken got drunk and opened his heart. I was grieved over his afflictions.

He looked at me and said, "Man, I was the best running back in Florida last year and now look at me. I'm nothing!"

I tried my best to be a friend because some things in life are bigger than football and this was one. I truly understood how he felt, wanting something so badly and being denied. That was the story of my life! He hugged me and staggered away. Chicken never regained his prominence at UCF and finally dropped out.

Meanwhile, I was budding into a local legend. I recall my first TV appearance on the Lou Saban show; I was so nervous. I said a prayer before going live on air. They asked a few questions and showed highlights. I was awarded player of the week, and recognized among the top rushers in Division II football. I was accomplishing fleets that I had always dreamt of. I scored ten touchdowns and ran nearly 800 yards in nine games. My teammates referred to me as the franchise, and I was considered an NFL prospect.

Nevertheless, I struggled academically. My courses were above my comprehension; I felt dumb. Sometimes I sat in class drawing pictures to waste time; I needed help. The coaches tried getting me a tutor but that didn't help; the work was too advanced. When I thought it couldn't get any worse, it did. Quickly, I earned a reputation of being a great football player, but a dumb jock. That affected my self esteem in the worst ways. One day, Coach Saban referred to me as an egg head. That was the final blow. I respected Coach Saban and for him to depict me in such a manner was painful. I drifted into depression and didn't know where to turn.

I needed help. God responded to me through a letter from my dad. Dad told me that he knew I was doing my best. He said to never give up because I am Christian and a believer in Jesus Christ. He inspired me to trust in God, and pray a little harder. I recited that letter on many occasions throughout life's hardships.

Shortly, Val came to visit me. I borrowed Teddy's car to pick her up from the bus station. She looked the same way that I had left her in Georgia, gorgeous. We shared quality time, postponing the inevitable. We both knew something was wrong. Time and distance had taken its toll on our relationship. Living apart with all the temptation of college was too much, even for us. When I drove her back to the bus station, I knew that our relationship was over.

It didn't take long before I met Felicia Nix. She was intriguing. I couldn't keep my eyes off of her during class. Shortly afterward, we started dating. We had the best of times as I tried my best not to think about Val. But she always found a way back into my heart. However, Val remained my friend and I love her even to this day. Meanwhile, Renita and I were becoming good friends. We talked about everything. She even tried to help me with my school work. I was grateful because I needed all the help that I could get.

Football season was over and I contemplated going home for the Christmas break, but I didn't have a clue how I would get there. Luckily I found a guy named Jack traveling to Jacksonville. Late, one Friday after finals, we headed home. The closer we got to Jacksonville the more nervous I became. I was really excited about seeing everybody. Finally, we made it to Jack's house just before dark. That's when I called mom and gave her directions to Jack's house. Minutes later, she and Stacy arrived. Mom opened her arms and embraced me; I wanted to cry. I couldn't believe how much Stacy had grown. She was seven years old.

It was good to be home. The sacred memories that were left behind awaited my return; I felt safe and secure. Dad and J anxiously anticipated my arrival. However, finding quality time to share with everyone became a dilemma. Somehow I managed to swing by the high school to see the basketball tournament. Everybody was there, it was jammed pack. I walked into the gym wearing my UCF paraphernalia. I didn't realize how popular I had become; my friends draped around me. It was nice to be important, but it's more important to be nice. I talked to the guys about college life, football, and responsibility. I was evolving into a leader without realizing it. Success obligated me to act responsibly whether I wanted to or not.

That next week mom and I went to Georgia. We had a great time until I got a disturbing call from school. It was Coach Davis telling me that I was academically ineligible; I had flunked out of college. My GPA dropped to a 1.9. It was alarming news, especially during Christmas. I didn't know how to tell mom, it would have crushed her. I pleaded and begged for a second chance. Coach Davis said he couldn't make any promises, but he would do his best and call back later. I envisioned my entire life going down the drain, the thought of telling dad was devastating. Everybody in the house knew something was wrong by the strange look on my face. I had no choice but to tell mom. She was traumatized. We sat on pins and needles waiting for Coach Davis to call. He had good news. I was reinstated back into school with certain demands. I had to make a 2.0 for the next couple of semesters.

I considered myself blessed and accepted the conditions. Daddy never knew how close I came to being kicked out of school. That would have destroyed him. God was certainly with me. When I returned to school, nearly half of my teammates had violated their academic probation and were dismissed from school. The stress of school was unbearable. If it had not been for the Lord on my side, I wouldn't have made it!

Many nights I sang gospel songs until I ran out of words to sing. I sang, "I don't feel no ways tired, I've come too far from where I started from; nobody told me that the road would be easy, I don't believe he's brought me this far to leave me." The more I sang, the more my spirit and faith was renewed. After singing, I prayed and meditated throughout the night until I fell asleep. Sometimes, I thought that I was beyond help, especially when my tutor failed. But the Lord prepared a table for me in the presence of my enemies. He anointed my head with oil until my cup ran over. Kenny taught me how to study by using mathematical and scientific strategies. Many nights we studied until the wee hours of the morning. I was four or five chapters ahead in my classes. This left more leisure time and helped me with my organization skills. At the end of that semester my GPA was a 2.6. What a relief! God came to my rescue over and over again. I turned my problems over to him. God had proven to me that he was my friend; he never abandoned me. Amen...

Teddy invited me to his home in Zephyrhills. I enjoyed meeting his family and getting away from Orlando; I needed a break.

Meanwhile, I had a surprise waiting for me back home in Jacksonville. Auntie and dad were acting strange; I knew they were up to something. When I arrived home, another Pinto was parked in the driveway! This time it was red. Auntie had bought me a new car. She said I was a good kid and she was proud of me. Words like that nurtured my self-esteem and inspired me to strive higher. I got all my favorite tapes and drove back to Orlando.

Felicia and I were getting better acquainted. That was bad news for Val, especially since we communicated less frequently. I confided in Renita, I needed someone to talk to. To my surprise, Renita was going through a similar predicament and we cried on each other's shoulders. Sometimes, we rode to Jacksonville together. Her parents always filled up the car with gas. It was their way of saying thanks.

Soon, my journey guided me into Tampa; that's where I spent unforgettable moments with Jack. It had been several months since I'd seen him. We punched each other in the stomach and wrestled; that's how we expressed our love. It was just like old times. Before exploring the town we shopped for groceries and decided on a salad. We carefully chose the freshest vegetables. Jack was a great cook, he prepared dinner. However, he experienced difficulty breaking the lettuce.

I took a good look at it and said, "Fool, no wonder. That's not lettuce its cabbage!"

We laughed until our stomachs cramped up. We were just a couple of college students trying to make it the best we knew how. We shared many funny moments like that.

Before I knew it, my freshman year of college was over. Wow, what a year! College was no joke. Despite mom and dad's plea, I decided to stay in Orlando for the summer. I searched for a roommate. Luckily, it didn't take long; I found the perfect guy Greg Atterbury; he was known as the "G-Man." I considered him to be a role model. G-Man was an NFL prospect and loomed larger than life. Many scouts attended practice to watch him. I asked him lots of questions about the NFL. Also he was a frat brother with Kappa Alpha Si. They were distinguished ambassadors that embraced the philosophy of unity and brotherhood. They accepted me as one of their own. G-Man and I roomed together in a two bedroom condo blocks away from campus. We jogged to campus in the smoldering heat with our shirts off. Some of the sorority sisters would distract us with provocative antics. But G-Man and I kept running; it was too hot to be thinking about girls.

Life was great, however, becoming an adult required demands. Greg and I had to find a job. I was a little nervous; I had never worked before. Coach Saban got us a job with Pepsi Cola. We labored on the assembly line assorting bottles from a conveyer belt. We worked at a rapid pace to prevent the bottles from falling. By the end of the day our hands were raw; we dreaded going to work. After working two days, G-Man and I had had enough; we quit. We walked out and didn't tell a soul.

The next day coach called us into his office. He was very disappointed. Coach said that I should have been courageous enough to resign in the proper manner. I felt ashamed, Coach Saban was absolutely right. G-Man and I had to find another job. Fortunately, it didn't take long. We signed up with a temp agency the next day. I was assigned to a soft metal company making parts. I had never worked on a machine before, but it didn't take long to learn. My only problem was staying awake, I got so sleepy. I even tried working with one eye closed; when that didn't work, I went into the bathroom and closed both eyes. After a couple of days, I was unemployed again.

I abandoned town and fled to Jacksonville. My family was delighted to have me home, but I felt like a stranger in town. Familiar places appeared foreign and my friends had vanished. Patiently, I absorbed time and worked on my car. I gave it a fancy coat of paint and dressed it with accessories. I drove aimlessly around town blasting Bob Marley. I had the prettiest Pinto in town. However, I had lost focus and stopped working out; that was a huge mistake.

When I wasn't preoccupied with my car, I worked as a handy-man around the house and ran errands; I enjoyed helping out.

I reported back to camp over weight and out of shape. I was in big trouble. The first person I saw was Darius Fore.

He said, "Man, you got bigger over the summer!"

When Coach Red saw me he said, "You look good, I hope you're ready, we're counting on you."

The first couple of days were always stressful because moving and unpacking was complicated, but I had no problems adjusting. I felt more comfortable compared to the previous year. The upper classmen taunted the freshmen and shaved their heads. Some tried to hide, but we always found them under the bed or in the closet. After a day of leisure, it was time for business. Class registration had begun. This time, I was much wiser about choosing classes.

Practice started abruptly with a conditioning test; I had to run seven laps in twelve minutes. I started fine until I reached my third lap; I knew that I was in big trouble. My extra weight was causing cramping and respiratory problems. I cradled my stomach and quit the run. I was ashamed, disgusted, and gasped for air. I felt faint and dizzy, and had to lie down. I had nobody to blame but myself. My teammates passed me one by one. I couldn't imagine what the freshmen must have been thinking after hearing so much about me; I was mortified. I wasn't the only player lying on my back, when I rolled over guess who I saw next to me? Teddy! That's right, Teddy Wilson. We were the two most valuable players out of shape and out of commission.

Coach Saban was very disappointed with me, but not nearly as much as I was with myself. I sat down on the bench looking befuddled. This sparked the beginning of my fall. Things would have been worse, if it weren't for Dennis Scott. He was the new wide receiver coach from Jesup, GA., mom's home town. His brother Lindsey Scott was an All-American wide receiver from the University of Georgia. Dennis and Lindsey were well respected and we considered them to be family. Suddenly, during practice I experienced severe cramps. This was nothing unusual. However, the cramps intensified and I was carted into the training room. My muscles constringed simultaneously and I fell to the floor in agonizing pain. The contractions quickly moved into my face and around my eyes and mouth, when I tried to speak my jaw cramped. Franticly, the trainers massaged my body. I lied lifeless on the floor and endured each cramp that tortured my body. I lost eleven pounds in less than three hours. After hours of agonizing pain, my body slowly responded to treatment. The trainers escorted me to my dorm room with ice bags in their hands. The first person to visit me was Dennis Scott. He said that he was concerned and just wanted to be by my side.

"Thank you Dennis for being more than a coach, but a genuine friend in my time of need." The training room became my second home. Just when I thought it couldn't get any worse, it did. Later that week, I suffered a devastating ankle injury. It was a toss left, suddenly there was a gaping hole. I made a sharp cut and rolled my left ankle over. I was in terrible pain. I'll never forget the disappointing expression on Coach Saban's face. He threw his cap down and stared angrily while grinding his teeth.

He paced back and forth like a caged lion kicking up patches of dirt. He yelled, "God Damn'it!"

It didn't take long for Aaron Sam and Robert Ector to fill in. In football, it's all about taking advantage of opportunity and that's exactly what they did. My ankle looked like a balloon and it was obvious that I would be out for a while. That was the last thing that I needed; a broken or sprained ankle days before the game opener. It was a slow healing process leading to an abbreviated season. I played in spurts, here and there. My best game that year was against Western Kentucky, I rushed for 107 yards. I compiled only 400 yards the entire season. However, I was well known and respected by opposing teams.

Sometimes, when we walked around the field for pre-game walk through, the opponents pointed and yelled, "That's him right there."

Some coaches offered me full scholarships if I would transfer to their schools. Regardless of their adulation the reality remained. Coach Saban's expression said it all; he'd look at my ankle and shake his head and mumble, "We're going to have to fix that ankle."

The next week we played against East Kentucky. Minutes before kick-off Coach Saban announced his resignation. There was an angry sigh amongst the team; some guys slammed their helmets down, others stood paralyzed.

Coach Saban looked at me and said, "Hey kid, you understand?"

I stood speechless feeling betrayed.

Despite giving a valiant effort we were defeated, and ended the season 2-9.

However, the other team that practiced at UCF finished the season with a much better record. The New Jersey Generals migrated south for training camp to avoid the violent winters. Herschel Walker and Doug Flutie proved to be a tremendous blessing for me. Both were Heisman Trophy winners in college. Ironically, one of them became my teammate in the National Football League. When I heard about the Generals coming, I felt the need to make a good impression. Herschel was my college idol and we played the same position. I watched him practice almost every day. One day after practice Herschel approached;

he was chiseled like a Greek God. I overcame my fear, swallowed my pride and introduced myself.

He shook my hand and said hello. I told him that I knew Lindsey Scott, his teammate at Georgia, and that his brother Dennis is a coach here. He looked surprised and smiled. He was a peaceful man of few words.

Herschel's teammate, Maurice Carthon, walked near and said, "Don't be late."

Then my mentor walked away. I talked to Herschel on many occasions. He was never loud or unprofessional. He carried himself like a true gentleman. One day, I sought his advice on improving my forty time. He told me to stay low and explode from my hips. His advice worked like a charm, and I reduced my forty time to a 4.3. I felt privileged to have known the best college player in the country, or perhaps of all time.

Doug Flutie defied logic; his stature was unintimidating. But, he was an amazing talent, dazzling opponents with acrobatic moves and "hail merry" passes. The press followed their every move, they were great ambassadors.

In spite of having a disappointing season, I finished with at 3.4 GPA; I even made the Dean's List! I was doing so well in school that I didn't have to attend study hall anymore. Suddenly, I felt that I could succeed in life without football.

However, no one was more influential that year than Rudy Gordon. He was a 29 year old freshman that was trying to resurrect a football career after returning from the military. Rudy and I had a lot in common, we shared a special bond. If you've ever had a close friend, then you know what I mean.

Meanwhile, Felicia and I kept a log on the fire. Our relationship got hotter and hotter. We went out on the town and had special moments like the time we went to Lakeland to see Luther Vandross. We had so much fun; I wish it could have lasted forever.

By now the season was over and it was time for recruiting. We didn't have a head coach, but we had to move forward. I'll never forget the weekend that Naz was scheduled to visit UCF. I was his host. They gave me lots of money and told me to show him a good time. I realized all colleges were guilty of extortion and under the table dealings. We partied at a club called Rosie O'Grady. All the pretty girls were there and I tried my best to show him the weekend of a lifetime. Nevertheless, Naz signed with North Carolina State.

Things were difficult at home, mom had lost her job. She robbed Peter to pay Paul. Finding a new job wasn't easy. Weeks later, mom was employed as a secretary at Spring Field Baptist Church; she hated it!

Things would have been better if she and Lenny were doing well. Lenny wasn't staying home, there was another woman. Soon, Lenny became a new father outside of his marriage. Mom was hurt, confused, angry, and broken hearted. I felt overwhelmed; dad's drinking problems and my academic woes were enough to push me over the edge! Instead, I dropped to my knees to beseech God's help. And like always he answered my call. He gave me peace in the middle of a storm; that was a clear sign. I told mom that everything would be alright; she cried and thanked me.

To help deal with stress, I went fishing. The tranquility of nature soothed my soul. However, Jack's presence on campus boosted my spirit and made me smile. I tried hooking Jack and Renita up but it didn't materialize. By now, it was spring break. Jack and I planned on going to Ft. Lauderdale. The trip was short, but we made sure to stop at our favorite restaurant, The Waffle House. I didn't need a menu; my favorite dish was a waffle with two scrambled eggs on the side. Jack ate anything. After demolishing his food, he had the audacity to stare at my plate and ask for a bite; I kept right on eating!

Ft. Lauderdale was unseasonably cold; our wardrobe rendered us vulnerable to the plummeting temperatures. Fortunately, we met a hot young lady; soon the temperature started to rise. She wanted to socialize later that night, but we needed another date to keep three from being a crowd. She told us not to worry. Jack and I were excited and must have done 300 push-ups to get buffed up before the girls arrived. Time quickly approached, and there was a gentle knock on the door. We paused and took a final look in the mirror. Jack slowly opened the door. Then, she gave him a big hug. Soon, her friend waltzed from around the corner, wearing a pink lace dress. Our chins dropped, she was huge! To make matters worse, she was my date! I could see Jack laughing from the corner of my eye. I couldn't believe my luck.

Suddenly, they went into the bathroom and came out with a change of heart. My date wanted to know if it was alright to switch dates. Before she got the words out of her mouth, I answered yes! Jack didn't say a word; he just looked stupid. Things had completely turned around; I stared at him and smiled. She tried to accost Jack with hugs and kisses, but he eluded her advances, running from one side of the room to the other. You should have seen them! It turned into a comedy show.

I shouted, "Jack told me he likes you!"

His date said, "I like him too, now give me a kiss!"

Jack said, "Gone now, gone."

It was hilarious. Jack eventually gave her a kiss before they left. We laugh about that to this day! That was a day I'll never forget.

I had many unforgettable memories; like the day I met Gale Sayers. I called dad when I heard he was coming to UCF. I made sure to be the first one there. Gale's tailored suit appealed to his physique; he looked great! Gale talked about an array of topics. But nothing was more captivating than his friendship with Brian Piccolo. I visualized his graceful runs, and dreamt of emulating his greatness. Gale was a man of tremendous faith, and his inspiring message rattled my soul. I realized that we shared a lot in common, and his presence strengthened my faith. I was delighted to introduce myself and shake his hand. I revered him as the most electrifying running back in NFL history. On that night, I rededicated my life to a higher purpose and sought to accomplish the unthinkable. I felt emancipated, and I ceased to look at men as trees. It became clear, that only God should be praised. Thank you Gale Sayers for helping me to accept the beautiful gifts within myself. And to Herschel Walker, thank you for helping me to increase my speed; your advice worked like a charm. And to Doug Flutie, you gave me hope that little guys could make it. I realized the size of a man's heart is what really mattered.

It wasn't long before my faith was placed on trial, but my character was exonerated. We ended the season with physicals. I thought it would be a quick routine check-up. I was surprised when Dr. Baker told me that I needed surgery on my left ankle. He explained that I had bone chips, and removing them required surgery; a procedure that involved inserting screws in my ankle to mend my tibia and fibula. I stood in shock and walked out deflated.

The night before surgery was agonizing. I tossed and turned, entertaining my greatest fears. I called for my trainer. Within minutes, Charlene had arrived to comfort me. Her reassurance rendered me a sigh of relief. Promptly at 4:30AM my phone rang. I had thirty minutes to get dressed and prepare myself before being chauffeured to the hospital. I left with my Bible in hand, and my duffle bag draped over my shoulder.

When I arrived at the hospital, I was bombarded with tons of paper work to fill out. It must have taken an hour. Shortly afterward, a nurse walked me to my room and instructed me to take off my clothes and put on a blue gown. I experienced a multitude of fear and anxiety before surgery. She noticed I was nervous, and gave me a pill to relax. It didn't take long before I felt better, I started laughing and telling jokes! I even asked if I could take some pills home. She laughed, but I was serious! Once on the operating table, the surgeon wasted no time. He drew lines on my ankle with a pen, indicating where he was going to make the incisions. As the Doctor inserted IV's into my arm I stared at the heart monitor; he told me to count from twenty quickly. The room turned black, and I felt myself fade away.

Waking up and hearing mom's comforting voice gave me hope. I couldn't say much though, the anesthesia hadn't worn off.

Suddenly, pain intruded into my ankle; the anesthesia was wearing off. At odd times of the night I was awaken to eat and take medication; I preferred sleeping. I was released from the hospital on Christmas Eve. Renita helped me to my feet; the pain was excruciating. It throbbed similar to a heat burn. Walking with crutches was a challenge. I stumbled through the door with a cast up to my knee. Renita and I loaded up the car and headed to Jacksonville for Christmas. Her words were compassionate and heartfelt; I never could have made it without her.

Back home, my needs were catered. However, the crutches began rubbing under my arm pits making them raw. So, I hopped around on one leg; it was faster and less painful. Time traveled lethargically and I remained incubated in bed. When I returned to school, I encumbered serious challenges. Getting around on campus was difficult, so daddy bought me a bicycle. I tied my crutches to the bike and draped my book bag across my shoulders. With my leg mounted in a cast it was frightening navigating around campus on my bike. I must have fallen a dozen times or more. Students tried to help me to my feet, but my pride wouldn't allow them. I was stubborn. The second problem was learning how to take showers without getting the cast wet. It took lots of practice but I did that too.

Shortly afterwards, Gene McDowell became our new football coach. He was an established defensive coordinator at Florida State, and was known for producing winning programs. Many of our coaches lost their jobs. Most of the guys were getting prepared for spring football, but I only attended meetings. I lost my starting position to Aaron Sam, a running back from Philly. This was not the time to be hurt, especially with a new coaching staff. I had to prove myself all over again, and this time it wouldn't be easy. Some of the guys decided to transfer to other schools; the thought crossed my mind. But my spirit felt at home, so I remained.

Final exams were close, both Kenny and I studied relentlessly. As a result, my grades substantially improved, and Kenny graduated with a degree in Marketing and signed a baseball contract with the Chicago White Sox. School ended, and it was time to remove my cast. I drove to the doctor's office and waited in the lobby. I sat patiently reading a magazine until Dr. Baker called me into his office. He searched for his utensils and grabbed a saw like tool, just like the doctor used when I broke my arm. The blade penetrated my cast and smoke fumigated the room. I barely recognized my ankle, it was small and scaly. I had a long road to recovery. But like always, the Lord sustained me. I began rehabbing my ankle in the hot whirlpool. Soon, I was able to walk comfortably without crutches. Sometimes when no one looked, I tried running. But my performance haltered, I wasn't ready. Persistently, I worked until there were signs of improvement. Dr. Baker felt my ankle was strong enough to remove the screws. He numbed the area and grabbed a knife, I trembled in my seat. Before making a small incision above my ankle, he warned me to sit perfectly still. I felt the screws coming out of my ankle one by one. Minutes later, I walked out with a slight limp and hoped for a speedy recovery.

The summer was all business; I had four months to get ready for training camp. I decided to stay in Orlando to prepare. My old friend Rudy and I roomed together. He lived in a four bedroom home on a lake. I often wondered how Rudy could afford a place like that while going to school. Rudy told me that Coach McDowell recruited him to Florida State but he chose the military instead. He was informed that Coach McDowell was the head coach at UCF and considered attending. He was persuaded with a house and an income.

Rudy made me feel right at home, we had tons of fun. He was a single father of three, and I admired his will to succeed. However, the stress of fatherhood became unbearable. Rudy slammed doors and verbally abused his kids. Soon, things took a turn for the worse and financial woes became our demise; our friendship disintegrated.

When I told mom and dad, they were really concerned. They came down to make sure I was fine. I had to find another roommate or go back to Jacksonville. Emma mentioned to Ronnie and Miller that I needed a place to stay. They didn't hesitate to ask me to move in. Miller was a manager and he helped me to get a job in the warehouse; I made $161 a week. I thought that I was rich! My job was simple; I loaded and unloaded plexi-glass. I looked forward to going to work; my coworker Tyrone showed me all the ropes. He didn't have a car, and I didn't mind taking him home after work. We sat in traffic jams while sweat dripped from our faces. Often I felt like leaving my car on the side of the road and catching a ride with someone that had air conditioning. It was the dog days of summer!

Miller and Ronnie were really nice. On weekends, Miller and I went fishing and Ronnie taught me how to cook my favorite Chinese dish, Egg Foo Young. I helped around the house as much as possible because they never charged me rent. That was my way of saying thanks. Three months had already gone and I decided to go home for the last month to see my family. Felicia and I had gotten well acquainted, and it was hard to say goodbye. We decided not to take our relationship any further because we were traveling in different directions.

Once in Jacksonville I joined the YMCA to get into peak shape before returning to training camp. When dad was injured back in high school, he swam for exercise, and that's what I did. My flexibility and strength improved drastically. My ankle felt normal and ready for the task at hand. One of the highlights of my summer was attending the Victory Tour with Renita and her sister. There was a barrage of screaming fans with tears in their eyes. Michael Jackson's electrifying ballads and unique dance ensembles hypnotized the audience. During the climax of the event, Robin mysteriously disappeared, and was camouflaged among the crowd. Renita and I were panic stricken, and desperately called for help. Minutes later, Robin returned unscathed.

Summer was passing quickly and so were my dreams of making the NFL. I approached another season with average stats, a new coach, and a bad ankle. A bleak prognosis to say the least; the odds were forged against me. My only hope was God's grace and mercy; that's all I needed.

The year was 1985 and I entered into my junior year. I was shocked to learn only five of the original fifty-two freshmen in 1983 returned. I viewed education through a different prism, and realized football wasn't a guarantee. My new roommate had the heart of a lion. We both were fierce competitors fighting for the same position. When I met Gil, he was sitting on the bed with his family members flanked around him; it was like déjà vu. He was short and well built. Gil was an outstanding running back from the Fort Myers area. After spending the first day talking and getting to know each other, I knew that he was a special guy. This time I was in great shape and my ankle had made vast improvements. Right from the start, I established myself as a team leader. However, earning my starting job back from Aaron Sam wouldn't be easy.

We practiced ruggedly and the physicality took its toll. My position coach was Allen Gooch, a former UCF player. He demanded that each athlete gave their best on and off the field. Right from the start I could tell things were different. That's exactly what we needed. It shaped us into men and it made us appreciate the simple things in life. I began getting ice baths in the whirlpool after every practice for preventative measures. Man that water was so cold, I could barely take it, but it kept my ankle and legs from getting fatigued.

Our fastest player was a junior college transfer. Bernard Ford became a dear friend and the Buffalo Bill's second round selection in the NFL draft. Bernard and Teddy terrorized opponents with their blinding speed. Our offensive coordinator retired with a Super Bowl ring with the Pittsburgh Steelers. Mike Kruczek designed his offense around a relentless passing attack. That spelled disaster for me; I rarely got the ball. Once, we threw 66 times in one game; a school record. Gil was sidelined with a neck injury and had to wear a brace. I felt really bad and adopted him as my little brother.

When his mom called, she said, "Take care of my baby." That's exactly what I did; I loved Gil. We had a lot in common. He was down to earth and just an all around great guy. His mom raised him well. Gil never traveled with the team but I became his biggest hero. He always prayed for my success.

By now, the season was in full swing and we were off to a rocky start. However, Teddy was having a stellar year. He went on to make All American with over 1100 yards and 76 catches. I struggled getting playing time. On the other hand, school was going great and I didn't have a worry about my grades anymore. I was a B student thanks to Renita. I didn't know how to type and that's where she came in; God bless her heart. She must have typed dozens of term papers for me. It was a big sacrifice because she had her own papers to type. She didn't charge me one single dime; that's when I really noticed what a sweet girl she really was. Renita had the total package; smart, beautiful, and spiritual. She knew exactly what she wanted out of life. She didn't have a boyfriend and I didn't have a girlfriend, the timing was perfect. From that moment on we were together day and night.

Renita supported me in every way and became one of my greatest fans. During one home game, I glanced into the stands and saw a big banner with my name on it saying, #44 no slowing down! Renita had someone make it; she really made me feel special.

Meanwhile, we were preparing for the biggest game of the season against our rival. Bethune Cookman was a fierce competitor, and we were considered a huge underdog. It was an exciting battle with several lead changes. With seconds to play and down by one point, we managed to come up with a big catch near field goal range. We had no choice but to try a 55 yard field goal, something that had never been done before. Everyone in the stadium stood on their feet in silence. The players and coaches on both sides were holding hands, it was hard to watch. The snap was perfect. Our kicker, Eddie O'Brian, went into the history books with a low squiggly kick that barely made it over the goal post. The crowd went wild and the players and coaches ran around the field in pandemonium. We rushed Eddie and jumped on his back, he was lost under a mould. He only weighed 150 lbs soaking wet; I'm surprised he didn't break in half. That game remains treasured. It became the greatest victory of my college career; it showed me how to achieve the impossible. We defeated a much superior team. It was like David and Goliath, no one gave us a chance. But with a smooth stone called faith we slew the Mighty Giant called Bethune Cookman Wild Cats.

However, the most significant memories were shared inside the locker room. Witnessing my teammates return from battle was truly amazing. Many suffered battle wounds and others wounded egos. Loud bellows echoed from the shower as water splashed against abrasions. Rarely did I finish a game healthy; I labored in agony. Nevertheless, the best part was laughing and celebrating the rare thrill of victory. However, we frequently experienced the agony of defeat. Some players threw their helmets across the room, others cursed like sailors. But no matter what happened in the locker room, it stayed there. We worked it out like men. Before leaving we prayed together as a team and walked out of the locker room with our heads held high.

After most games, I left with dad and Emma to visit Emma's daughter Gloria. They never stayed long because J was left in Jacksonville alone. With each game my pain and discomfort escalated, that opened a door I hated to go through (pain pills). The team trainer gave me endless supplies of 800 milligram Motrin to eliminate pain and inflammation. Sometimes, I could barely walk, but I had to be ready for the next practice. Motrin was the only solution. I became addicted to pain pills; I took ten a day. I was under a tremendous burden to excel in order to make it to the next level, the NFL. The game I loved as a child was slowly turning political. Each game that we lost jeopardized jobs and scholarships. To attract marquee players, some of my teammates were allegedly compensated. Sometimes, the alumni contributed money and many illegal perks; I was in awe.

Meanwhile back home, mom was having a difficult time finding a job. Times were getting tougher by the minute. She lost her car and was catching different rides to work odd jobs. I hated to see bad things happen to such a beautiful person, mom never complained. She just did her best. I went home because I felt mom needed me in some way but maybe she didn't quite know how to ask. I recommended that she keep the Pinto, she needed it much more than I. As much as I loved that car, it was easy giving it to her. It was the least I could do. I believed if we continued obeying and serving God that he would bless us with bigger and better things. Daddy admired me and declared that God would bless me for what I'd done. Already, I'd felt blessed and never looked for anything in return. I rode back to Orlando with Renita she had purchased a new car; a Chevy Chevette. It was disappointing not seeing my Pinto in the parking lot, but Renita gave me a set of keys to her car; my blessings had begun.

Renita and I were undecided on choosing a college major. We pondered many options, however, none were appealing. Renita's roommate suggested pursuing a lucrative career in advertising. It sounded nice; we were persuaded. We took many classes together and spent quality time on the weekends. We enjoyed dining in buffet restaurants; we made sure to eat our monies worth. I walked out looking six months pregnant! There were times we fished in nearby lakes; watching Renita take the fish off the hook was hilarious. But nothing was more gratifying than attending church service together; it was the source of our strength.

I recognized UCF as my home away from home and I considered my friends to be family; especially my teammates. Throughout the years, I watched some evolve into responsible young men, while others struggled. That's where I came in. My childhood past thoroughly prepared me to be a role model to many of them. I was respected by my teammates, coaches, and peers. They even protected Renita in my absence and treated her like a big sister. Sometimes, I cooked special treats for Gil; he was my dawg. On most occasions we chilled and listened to music.

Meanwhile, the end of the semester drew nigh. Again, I had another disappointing season with only four or five hundred yards rushing and a couple of touchdowns, nothing to brag about. I was going in the wrong direction after having such a strong freshman campaign. However, my grades were exceptional, and that's what really mattered.

One day during practice, I leaped to catch a pass. I heard a loud click from my knee. The pain was excruciating. I had never experienced anything like it before. My knee had swollen, it resembled a balloon. Discretely I walked off the field to inform my coach about my injury; he didn't believe me. He accused me of being lazy and trying to skip practice; I was offended. I was tired of being injured and taking Motrin; it appeared I had a plague. Just when I thought it couldn't get worse it did. I had to have another surgery; this time on my knee; I was broken hearted. I figured that this was the end of my career, because previous players that sustained knee surgery never regained their form. The good news, it was only a scope to remove torn cartilage.

Dad and mom didn't take the news well. Lenny told me to repent of my sins. But I couldn't recall any bad deeds to mind. What was God telling me? I was puzzled. I began reading my Bible and waiting for answers. The next day Renita drove me to the hospital. Registration was much easier because my paperwork was on file. I even had the same nurse prepping me for surgery. She told me not to make coming in for surgery a habit; I couldn't have agreed with her more. I asked her if I was going to get another pill to make me feel good again, she laughed. A few hours later, I woke up with three tiny holes around my knee where the instruments were inserted. It didn't require a cast, but my season was over.

My treatment was ice and rest, and oh yeah, Motrin. The first night was restless; I tossed and turned. However, the pain gradually subsided. That was the last surgery I required as an athlete. Nevertheless, I was a little depressed. I went home that weekend while the team played on the road. Mom and dad gave me lots of love and that's just what I needed. Dad was surprised to see me maneuvering without crutches. He expected me to be in a cast or in a wheelchair. I spent time reminiscing with him and J before traveling back to Orlando.

Without football, I had lots of time to reflect on my life. I gained a lot from those private moments; I needed time to reconnect with God. I was certain that God was preparing me for a higher purpose. I had every reason to quit and blame God but I didn't. I was inspired to pray and work harder. I refused to be denied of my dreams and goals. I was at war and I intended to fight back!

I started by writing down my goals, beginning with football. The ultimate goal for most football players is playing in the NFL, especially with millions of dollars on the line. It was no different for me, and I started prioritizing my life around football.

After the season, I met with Coach McDowell. He told me that I had the ability to play on the next level. However, I wasn't a Herschel Walker or Tony Dorsett but I was in that next class. Also, he was proud of my progress in class and he wanted me to take more of a leadership role. I left feeling encouraged knowing that I was on the right road. I needed to get bigger and remain healthy, so I started a rigorous off-season training program. Soon, I gained 10 lbs of muscle and increased my bench press to over 450 lbs and squatted over 600 lbs. I became one of the strongest players on the team. My hard work ethic gained everybody's respect, including the coaches. They saw a young man committed and dedicated. My transformation forced the coaching staff to commit to a running game. I became the primary focus without setting one foot on the field. My name began to circulate among NFL scouts; my future looked promising.

Spring football started with mat drills at 4:30AM. Practice was intense and required peak stamina. It was the ultimate test for teamwork and dedication. We submitted to a series of drills designed to increase flexibility and strength; it wasn't for the weak and weary. Some threw up, and others laid down complaining of faint. We finished drills by climbing a thirty foot rope. Frequently, I motivated my teammates with spirited chants and high fives. After drills, Gil and I rushed to breakfast and hit the sack before class. After about three weeks of mat drills it was time to hit the practice field.

Quickly, I set the tempo by busting people in the mouth. I played with a vengeance. My performance lured the attention of everybody. I was no longer denied. Coach named Aaron and I as starters. Finally, I was back where I belonged. My storms had ended and the sea was calm. Our spring practice culminated into a scrimmage. It was greatly anticipated, and hordes gathered in attendance. The offensive and defensive teams taunted one another in battle. I received the football and ran towards the sideline; we called it I Right 49 Pitch. Aaron blocked the linebacker. Quickly, I hit the hole and collided with Wyatt Bogan, our 6'3", 250 lb All-American inside linebacker. Wyatt fell on his back. I stumbled a bit and regained my balance running 80 yards for a touchdown! It was one of the team's greatest runs.

Coach McDowell stopped practice and called the team together and said, "That's a football player. Son, you can go in!" I jogged off the field; my teammates honored me with applause. That was one of the proudest moments of my life. I became a hot topic around campus.

School was nearly over and I prepared for finals; I was determined to make the deans-list. College exposed me into a new world of unique and cultivating experiences. New friendships emerged, extending beyond city limits; I loved it! My confidence soared, and many rare opportunities surfaced from behind the horizon. Getting my degree became essential. However, I wasn't scheduled to graduate on time, I needed more credit hours. Attending summer school was my only option. With less than a year to graduate I was terrified. I enrolled in extra classes to accelerate the pace of graduation. The work was intense, especially algebra; I hated it! Nevertheless, I managed to balance my time and enjoy special moments with Renita.

Renita and I went to Miami with another couple, Marcus and Sondra; college friends that we knew well. The next week we were in the Florida Keys. It was beautiful, coconut and mango trees littered

Dade County. Renita and I had so much fun. We fished overnight on the bridge. She caught the first fish, a Red Snapper; we showed everyone when we got back to campus. In spite of so much traveling, my grades were great in math. I earned a B and came closer to earning my degree.

The summer was coming to an end, and I got a job through the athletic department. I worked with one of my teammates as a janitor. It was the easiest job in the world, because we did absolutely nothing. Sometimes after emptying the trash we took turns napping in the closet. The coaches didn't seem to mind and neither did we. The coaches loved the idea that I was on the campus working out and going to school. Coach Gooch and I watched games and analyzed my performance. I learned football wasn't only physical but also mental. That was the missing piece of my game. Now, I was complete.

Before the final week of school, Renita and I watched the NBA finals between the Houston Rockets and the Boston Celtics. It was a great series, but we hated the Celtics. Every time Houston scored we'd jump up and scream. Boy, those were the best years of my life, I tell ya! I hated leaving summer school. But, I needed to go to home for a couple of weeks to see my family before camp started. When I arrived home, mom told me that she had been robbed on her job at gun point, and she feared the worst. I could hear the pain in her voice. I was enraged, but I thanked God that she was safe.

J was 86 years old, and the thought of her dying plagued my mind. I hated those thoughts. Nevertheless, she was hanging on. J and I savored every precious moment. She loved eating fresh water Brim. We fried them crispy and ate the bones; it didn't get any better than that.

Sports enthusiasts inquired about my status in the upcoming draft; they knew that the time was quickly approaching. The stress of being drafted into the NFL raised anxiety and tension; my remarks were evasive. However, spending time with Jack relieved my stress and eased my burdens. Our expression of brotherhood demonstrated the epitome of friendship; Jack was a rare commodity.

I started football camp with one thing in mind. I wanted to be the best running back in America and the first player drafted into the NFL from UCF. Those were awfully big goals, but I've always thought big and furthermore, I was 208 lbs benching over 450 lbs and running 4.3 forty. Those stats were as good as any in the nation. My greatest dilemma was playing at a small Division II school with no media exposure and a personal challenge to remain healthy. I finished camp injury free for the first time thanks to a strong off season conditioning program, a better diet and better living. I was also voted team captain. Gil and I made sure to get plenty of water and rest between practices.

We were eager to play our home opener against our arch nemesis Bethune Cookman. Our returning line up was among the nation's best, and our performance was spectacular. Quickly, the offense established dominance with time consuming drives. My game winning touchdown sealed the victory. Surprisingly, J was in attendance. She sat in the handicap section with dad and Emma flanked by her side. I was happy to see her.

I appeared on nearly every sports and news show in Central Florida. The publicity lured the attention of a local sports agent. Phil Williams wrote me letters each week. He praised my efforts and discussed his services. Soon, letters from the NFL and CFL cluttered my locker; I was shocked!

I occupied my leisure time visiting pet shops. I loved it! Sometimes Renita and I would stay for hours. I took a special interest in birds, especially parrots. However, they were too expensive, so I settled for a cockatiel. I named him Mister. He became everybody's favorite, especially Gil. Mister whistled a sexy tune whenever Gil walked by his cage. Mister was easy to train and he said at least twelve words. His favorite was "fire it up!"

Meanwhile, we lost three consecutive games; I hated losing. Practice became long and tedious. Our team needed a sparkle. I was surprised to find out that it wouldn't come from a player but rather a bird, Mister.

Somehow the athletic department got the news about Mister and called Sports Illustrated. They loved the story. The next day Sports Illustrated called and interviewed me about Mister. Soon, Sports Illustrated was knocking on my door. An entourage of photo journalists greeted me. I was nervous, but the ambiance was smoothing. I discussed the story with the editor and he came up with a slogan. The headline read, "UCF Needs to Fire It Up!" But there was only one problem, Mister had gone away. The publicity about Mister alarmed the dormitory administration. Rules clearly stated that pets were prohibited in the dorms. Mister went to Jacksonville to live with mom. My hands were tied and so were Sports Illustrated. Cleverly, we returned to the pet store and borrowed a cockatiel that resembled Mister; our problem was solved. Photo shoots started promptly, I changed into my uniform and posed with the bird on my shoulder, just like a movie star. I must have taken two or three hundred shots. The attention quickly drew a big crowd. It was hard to fathom that Sports Illustrated was at UCF doing a story on me!

The story was greatly anticipated and scheduled to run two or three weeks later; I was excited. I received a disturbing phone call. Regrettably, Sports Illustrated had to cancel the story; Mister's replacement led to a conflict of interest. It was a big disappointment. No one felt worse than mom. Shortly after she called to inform me that Mister was dead.

While she was out, the pest control sprayed inside of the house and contaminated Mister's water; it was a tragic loss. Nevertheless, I had to focus on what was ahead. We were mid way through the season and the team was on a winning streak. However, dad was acting bizarre. His eyes were dilated and he spoke with a slur. Before leaving the game, he stared and mumbled, "I love you son." I knew something was terribly wrong; I began to worry.

Meanwhile, I received more letters from well known agents. Nick Kick was notoriously popular among southern players; we met at UCF to talk business. He drove a beautiful BMW. I asked Nick if he could get me a car like that. He told me not to worry, that he'll get me any car I wanted. During this time, Renita and I barely got a chance to see each other. We always found a way to make late night rendezvous at 7-11 to play our favorite game, Pac-Man. I played so much that the joy stick made my fingers raw. I made a vow that if I ever made enough money I would buy a Pac-Man machine for my house.

My stock was rising, I became a hot commodity. My daily activities became an interest to the local media. I was featured on a special sports edition entitled, "A Bright Light is Shining at UCF!" It was an extreme honor. Around 5:30AM I was disturbed by a loud commotion outside of my dorm; it was rowdy reporters assembling their equipment against the door. After greeting the cast I was ensued by bright lights around campus. Inquisitive minds lingered closely behind.

My success had spread rapidly, and lured the attention of a sports agency in Chattanooga, TN. I was serenaded in a beautiful mansion that sat majestically on countless acres overlooking the open plains. The house was enameled with gold and precious metals. Despite the agencies enormous wealth, I differed my options to Nick Kish and Phil Williams. I was really proud of myself.

Three days before my final game, I endured a devastating injury in practice. I felt a peculiar pain in the back of my leg; I pulled a hamstring. I couldn't bear the thought of telling coach and disappointing my teammates; I suffered quietly. My only hope of playing was to receive treatment and take extra Motrin.

My last game was against a small school called Samford College. Finally, it dawned on me, I was playing my last college game. As the tears rolled down my cheeks, I sat beside my locker and stared as my teammates prepared for battle. Coach McDowell called the team together and gave us a motivational speech. He assured me that several NFL scouts were in attendance. My heart fell to my knees because I was hurt and unable to perform my best. I found a quiet place and prayed for a miracle. Then I wrapped my hamstring with an ace bandage and went out on faith. I stretched and warmed up before kick-off, however it had no effect on the piercing pain. It felt like a charley horse, but five times worse. I didn't know what to do; I was in no condition to play. Nevertheless, I finished the game with 116 yards on just three carries! Somehow I scored a 79 yard touchdown; the longest run from scrimmage in school history, a record that stood for 21 years. I was honored on the sideline by zealous teammates.

Coach McDowell said, "Son, that was a great run."

We ended our season that night as winners. It was my greatest

run; too bad daddy missed it. Daddy never missed a game in thirteen years. However, he heard the play on the intercom as he walked into the stadium. Better yet, daddy saw me end my final college game as a winner. I never could have done it without his help. Thank you so much dad!

The following Monday the team assembled and recognized the seniors for their contributions. It was hard concealing my emotions, but I saluted my teammates with grace and humility. I commended the coaches for cultivating my passion and nurturing me into a quality young man. Also, I acknowledged the underclassmen and encouraged them to be ambassadors of freedom. I took off my jersey and presented it to Gil. He received it with tears in his eyes and promised to wear it with honor. The room exploded with a thunderous applause and I was accosted with love. I realized it was over and slowly walked away carrying with me my dignity, my pride, and my future.

I finished my career with honors, and had compiled nearly every rushing record in school history. But my real challenge was yet to come. The NFL workouts were right around the corner and I feared rupturing my hamstring. Immediately, I received treatment. Soon my discomfort dissipated and I jogged in the cool crisp night of winter. I anticipated receiving an invitation to play in the upcoming bowl games. NFL prospects were invited to play in order to be evaluated by NFL coaches. I never got a call, my pride was wounded. However, the most critical evaluation was the NFL scouting combine, a weekend of drills and tests to determine a player's draft status. I didn't make that trip either; I was baffled. I sat home rejected watching the combine on TV as my competitors secured their stock in the NFL. I was embarrassed to face my community, and avoided any questions pertaining to the draft; I was livid! My ambition to become the first UCF player drafted into the NFL appeared bleak.

No matter how gloomy it appeared, I couldn't lose hope. The following week I received a call to report to the athletic building at 2PM. An NFL scout from the Cleveland Browns wanted to see me. I almost jumped through the roof!

"Yes! Yes! Yes!" I screamed, but it wasn't a time to celebrate. It was already 1PM and I needed to concentrate mentally and psychologically before leaving. Quickly, I massaged my muscle with Icy-Hot; then I prayed. I gathered my tights, a couple of towels, and my new shoes mom bought and stuffed them into my duffle bag. Before leaving Gil told me that I could do it; he boosted my confidence. I was extremely nervous, this was my first time working out for the NFL, and I didn't know what to expect. It was a long walk to the athletic building. Yet, when I reflected on how far I had come since a little boy, I realized that I had nothing to lose. I was a winner from the very beginning; I was born with a destiny and nothing could change that. Not even the Cleveland Browns.

My performance was astounding; I ran a 4.37 forty, jumped vertical 41 inches and broad jumped 10'3". I was promised at least a free agent contract. He shook my hand and said he'd be in contact. Over the next three weeks I ran for several scouts. After running a 4.36 forty, the Tampa Bay Buccaneers scout and running back coach, Sylvester Croom, told me that I should be a high draft pick and would love to have me. The Pittsburgh Steelers said that if I ran anything close to a 4.3 I would be gone by the third round, I ran a 4.41, I knew in my heart that I had secured a spot in the National Football League. My stats were among the nation's best. Running on natural grass impeded my forty times. Nevertheless, my stats exceeded most of my competitors who ran on artificial turf.

I was running for a different team every other day. I was exhausted and needed a break. Every time I turned on the TV or read the newspaper, I saw predictions about the upcoming draft. My name was never mentioned; I was stressed. So for a little rest and relaxation I took a getaway with Gil to his home town. As the sun dawned upon endless orange groves, hues of amber illuminated the city. Gil's family had had about six trees in their yard. I spent most of my time there picking oranges. I was in paradise!

Gil's mom was the perfect host. She stocked the house with our favorite foods and made me feel right at home.

After Ft. Myers we decided to go hunting with friends; I enjoyed experiencing new challenges. Early one Saturday morning we all headed out in a pick-up truck. Gil and I sat in the back bed. It was freezing! It must have been in the 30's. We sat bundled up together under a blanket. The thought of a warm bed back at the dorm didn't seem like a bad idea. But I was a team player so I sucked it up and took the cold like a man!

After two hours of bone chilling torture, we finally made it and started our walk into the woods. We looked for anything that moved. I had a twelve gage shotgun, it had a serious kick. We walked miles without food or water; I was starved. Gil was beginning to look like a nice meal! Luckily, a flock of quail appeared about twenty yards ahead. Our opportunity for a kill was fading; the brush was only yards away.

One of the guys asked, "How many do you want me to shoot?"

Gil and I looked at him and said, "Fool, shoot as many as you can and hurry!"

Unfortunately, we had the wrong pellets and had to quickly reload the gun. Now the quail were feet away from the brush; we had to hurry. We fumbled nervously with our rifles until each quail disappeared into the brush. I yelled, "Shit!"

We left that day without firing one shot, then hopped in the pickup and headed for McDonalds; I ate two Big Macs. I've never gone hunting again.

The most memorable moment occurred during spring break in Daytona Beach. The black college reunion was the nation's most anticipated event among small black colleges. Over 300,000 students attended. Many lewd and lascivious activities were performed in public.

friend. I invited Renita to Boston. She thought it was a splendid idea, but I had to discuss the idea with mom; I valued her opinion. After addressing her concerns she gave me her blessing. However, it wasn't easy convincing Renita's parents; they preferred Renita being engaged, and I embraced their concerns, but I intended to propose to her at a later time. Sometimes Renita would weep; she was torn between me and her family. However, she was an adult, and the final decision was up to her.

Later that week Renita flew into Logan airport. I arrived hours before her flight; I didn't want to be late. I waited patiently until her plane had landed. Soon, the boarding area became congested as friends and family members anticipated seeing their loved ones. I stood afar twiddling my thumbs. Suddenly, the passengers entered the lobby; they were ambushed with joyful kisses. Renita walked gracefully from among the crowd. She was elegantly dressed, but burdened with luggage in her hand. She came to an abrupt halt and combed the horizon. But my identity remained camouflaged within the crowd. Quickly, the gathering dispersed and Renita and I gazed into each other's eyes; it was a defining moment. She acknowledged me with a smile, dropped her bag, and ran into my arms with tears in her eyes. Gently, I wiped away her tears with my shirt and greeted her with a kiss. That was the happiest moment I had had while I was in Boston.

It was wonderful having Renita with me; she transformed my life. Renita was my lover and my best friend; she was a blessing from God. Our favorite eatery was called the <u>No Name Restaurant</u>; they served the best seafood in town. Soon, my house turned into a home, and the NFL lifestyle became appealing.

However, my soul cringed when I considered mom and dad's afflictions; I felt compelled to help. But money couldn't solve dad's problems. Some nights he'd call weeping; I was deeply grieved. Sometimes I cried too; it eased the pain, and Renita was there to stop the hemorrhaging.

The next day rendered joy. I was enticed by a TV commercial to visit the BMW dealership in Warrick, Rhode Island; the new model had just arrived. Many consumers were lured into the dealership searching for their dream car. Suddenly, a familiar face emerged and walked towards me. it was Barry Havener, and old college teammate at UCF. I was astonished! Enthusiastically, we celebrated being reunited; he looked great! Barry had been working as a salesman for the dealership for years. He had been following my career and congratulated me on making the team. Barry was extremely proud. He took me around the dealership and introduced me to his colleagues. I confided to Barry that I couldn't get financed. He smiled and placed his arm around my shoulder and said "Don't worry. You choose the car and I'll finance it."

I felt like a child in a candy store. There were so many nice cars; I didn't know where to start. Barry told me to follow him. I had no idea where we were going. Suddenly, we approached a crowd. They were preoccupied admiring a vehicle displayed on the showroom floor. A black 325is flattered my imagination; it was adorable. I proceeded forward and noticed my reflection repelling against the glossy paint. The interior was flawless and the smell of new leather tantalized my senses. I fell helplessly in love, and I inquired about the cost. Barry said it was $28,500 and asked if I could afford it. I asked if he could reduce the price for an old friend. He chuckled and told me to fill out the paperwork.

The process was tedious. Renita and I waited in the office for a response. Suddenly, Barry appeared with a grim look on his face; I feared the worst. Then he erupted with joy and shouted, "You're approved! You're approved!"

I clinched my fist and gave Renita and Barry a hug. Barry walked towards the door; suddenly he turned around and said, "By the way, I took $4,000 off the price."

I was very grateful. On November 9, 1987, I purchased my first automobile. As I prepared to leave Barry walked me to my new car. But I was delayed by inquisitive customers that demanded a peep inside. They were oblivious to the fact that I had purchased it. Two of Barry's coworkers opened the glass showroom doors and asked everyone to step back. Barry cranked the engine; it purred like a cat. Slowly, he drove the car outside and relinquished it into my possession. However, I faced a major dilemma. I forgot how to drive a stick shift. I was embarrassed to ask for help, but my pride surrendered. Barry gave me a crash course in driving a stick in the parking lot. The entire dealership came out to watch. After a couple of attempts, my confidence was restored. Then something remarkable happened, it started to snow! I left the dealership skipping and stalling until I reached the front gate; it was the funniest thing. Renita followed cautiously behind me in the rental car. I saw her giggling at me out the rear view mirror. As I left, I waved goodbye to my old friend. That was the last time I saw Barry.

Nothing came easy that night. Waiting at the top of hilly roads for the stop light to turn green was terrifying. The car rolled backwards, barely missing the cars behind me. Other times, I stalled in traffic and angry motorists blew their horns. One man came to help me; God bless him. I would have still been there today without his help. I came to the conclusion that buying a stick shift wasn't such a bright idea. Either I was going to destroy the car or get into an accident. By now, I was in the middle of a snowstorm and visibility was minimal. My only hope was to make it to the highway and remain in 5th gear until I reached home. It wasn't easy, especially crossing two major intersections. With only a few miles to go, I said a quick prayer and took my chances.

I surged into my complex shortly after midnight. I parked in front of my window and stared at my car throughout the night. Driving to practice the next practice the next morning was hazardous. Sheets of ice blanketed the road, and I sled uncontrollably across the road. It was God's grace and mercy that protected me from harm.

The season was moving at a rapid pace and the holiday season was upon us. Renita and I looked forward to cooking Thanksgiving dinner. Coach Berry gave the players a day off to enjoy with our families; it was a rare treat. A memo circulated around the locker room for the players to order their free turkey's at a local poultry farm. The rookies were extremely excited and were among the first to order.

Renita purchased all of the turkey stuffers to go along with the meal. We drove to a distant location miles into the country to claim our turkey. However, the owner appeared confused. Suddenly, there was a snicker from behind the door, and a couple of veterans ran out with a video camera in their hand. It was a prank, and we turned out to be the real turkeys for Thanksgiving; but that was life as a rookie.

The temperatures in November plummeted well below freezing, and practice became unbearable, especially around sunset. We bundled together to defend ourselves against the treacherous weather; our uniforms offered little comfort. Weather conditions were so brutal that I felt like quitting. Most guys rubbed Vaseline on their faces to keep their lips and faces from cracking. Fortunately, our next game was in Miami; it was the closest thing to paradise. We embraced the tropical weather. The team arrived in south Florida a week prior to the game to get acclimated to the blistering heat. Coach Berry took winning seriously and he did his best to make sure we were prepared. I had no problems adjusting to the heat, but most of my teammates suffered from heat cramps; but after a day or two they were fine. Our team had recovered from the repercussions of the NFL strike and the blistering heat to form a cohesive bond.

I was really happy. Renita and I evolved our relationship to a higher plateau; I knew that she was the one she stood by my side during the good, bad, and ugly. Before I became an NFL player, Renita was there. She loved me unconditionally; I was truly blessed. However, the advances of attractive women were tempting. Most NFL players were easy targets, but I prayed for strength and the will to remain faithful. I considered my best option was to get married and dedicate my life to the woman I loved. So, I talked to God, mom, and dad; all three gave me their approval. The next week, I bought Renita an engagement ring, and I got a gold necklace with a patriot charm. I was ready to become a family man, but I wanted a sacred place to propose.

Unexpectedly, Renita decided to go back home for Christmas, and my instincts suggested that she was feeling insecure and doubted my level of commitment. She never said it right out, but I could tell by some of the comments that she made. Shortly after dusk, I drove her to the airport. She experienced an emotional breakdown and cried uncontrollably. I steered the car with one hand and wiped her tears away with the other. I searched for a safe location on the side of the road and pulled over. Gently, I held her in my arms and looker into her eyes and asked, "Will you marry me?"

Renita was speechless, her face glowed and her hands trembled. Soon, she gained her composure and grabbed my hand. She smiled and shouted, "Yes!"

I was the happiest guy on earth. Slowly, I presented the ring and placed it on her finger. It was worthy of a celebration. Unfortunately, Renita had a plane to catch.

Her plane was punctual, and passengers had already begun boarding. I held her in my arms until the final call. Saying goodbye was difficult, but we looked forward to sharing a lifetime together. I watched her walk away and stare at her ring. She turned her hand in different angles to capture a perfect sparkle. Before boarding, Renita glanced back and waved goodbye. As quickly as she had come to Boston, she had gone. I reflected on my family's reaction to my departure and sympathized; this time the shoe was on the other foot.

Meanwhile, we struggled for a playoff berth, each game was critical. The game against the Dallas Cowboys in Foxboro was very special. My high school teammate played for the Cowboys. I stood directly on the 50 yard line and honored the national anthem. Kelvin Martin stood opposite me, we engaged into a stare down.

It was a hard fought contest with several lead changes. The game ended without a decisive winner and was forced into overtime. Herschel Walker quickly ended any last minute heroics with an astonishing touchdown run for the Dallas Cowboys. It was a costly defeat.

We suffered our most devastating defeat against the Philadelphia Eagles. It was a perfect day in Foxboro, fall temperatures invaded Sullivan stadium in front of a sold out crowd. To assure a victory we needed big plays from our special teams; that's where I came in. I returned four kick-offs for 111 yards. Dad said I resembled Gale Sayers. On kick-off coverage I was a heat seeking missile hitting anyone with a different color jersey. I collided head first with a defender; suddenly, everything went black. The awful smell of ammonia jarred me conscious. My teammates helped me to my feet, and the fans cheered as I galloped to the bench. I stared at the Jumbo-Tron and it was a picture of me. I enjoyed stealing the attention of thousands in the stadium and millions throughout the nation. Daddy told me that I gave him a scare; he feared the worst. To make matters worse, I sprang my ankle. As a result, I missed three consecutive games. Nevertheless, Tony Franklin

missed three field goals that would have won the game. It was that kind of year...so close, yet so far.

The most rejuvenating moment was seeing daddy; he gave me hope. Gale Sayers was in attendance, but I never had a chance to thank him for those words back at UCF. That was the only game daddy attended that year. Dad enjoyed mingling with the players. They made an everlasting impression, and he raved about it for years. We explored the treasures of the outer banks of Boston and gorged ourselves on lobster at <u>No Name Restaurant</u>. Regardless of how much fun we had, dad always found ways to get a drink. It dampened my spirit because one drink turned into another. During his stay he had drunk a 5th of Gin. I tried not to worry, but I was scared from the past and feared the worst. The next day we arrived at the bus station. I tried to persuade daddy to fly, but he was afraid, and decided to ride the Peter Pan bus back home.

We missed the playoffs and ended the season with an 8-7 record. The Denver Broncos defeated us in the season's finale. The organization was highly disappointed and expected a playoff berth. But, there was next year; we had to think optimistically.

We concluded the season with a team meeting and medical evaluations. Some players remained in Foxboro until they were medically cleared; others were out of town before sundown. I preferred leaving town sooner than later, so I gathered my belongings and stuffed it into my BMW, and headed south. I left Boston with $30,000 cash in my pocket. I supplied myself with a bag of snacks and an array of tapes for the journey. I wanted to arrive home expeditiously; New Years Day was approaching and my relatives were anxious to see me. I made brief stops along the way to refuel and take bathroom breaks. I'd driven to Washington D.C. without a wink of sleep. I was exhausted and decided to lodge in a hotel. I enjoyed a peaceful sleep. I woke up rejuvenated and ready to eat a hearty breakfast before hitting the road.

Soon, I made it into South Carolina, then Georgia. The familiar appearance of Pine Trees littered the land. It was a sure sign that I was in the south. I recognized signs I had seen as a child. I maximized the volume and raced on I-95 listening to Michael Jackson. Jesup was less than an hour away. Soon, the reek odor of Rayonier Paper Factory welcomed me to Jesup; finally, I had made it.

My arrival into town caused a ruckus; folks carried on like I was the President of the United States. I took a short cut onto Fourth Street, hoping to remain anonymous; my plan worked like a charm. I approached the house with suspense. Holiday tunes exuded from within, followed by provoking laughter; it sounded like a party. I invited myself in through the back door and yelled, "Surprise!"

I caught everyone off guard. When they recognized me it was pandemonium! I received a hero's welcome! There were many questions about the NFL and life in the big leagues. The doorbell rang constantly; fans came over to welcome me home. I felt honored. Later, we cooked on the patio and ate our favorite foods. It was a great way to bring in the New Year. In the aftermath, I walked into the bedroom reminiscing about my unusual experiences in life. I felt humbled and unworthy of God's blessings. I knelt to my knees and thanked him. It was nice seeing loved ones; it reminded me about what was really important.

The next morning I arrived in Jacksonville, but things were different. I couldn't find home; mom and Lenny had divorced. I drove to our old house anyway, just for one last look; it was the only place I called home. I turned off my headlights and stared at the house from across the street. I thought about all of my childhood memories, and wondered if the words, <u>Chicago Bears Here I Come</u> were still on the back of my bedroom door. I thought about draft day, when I listened to U-2. I began crying as I said goodbye to a piece of my heart that was left inside.

Frantically, I searched for momma's new place; her apartment was on Harts Rd. I'll never forget the night I drove to her apartment. I walked precariously to the front door, my heart beat like a drum. I didn't know what to expect; I held my breath and knocked gently. I didn't know what to expect when I walked inside.

Suddenly, momma asked, "Who is it?"

I replied, "It's me momma!"

I knew that she was fine by the sound of her voice. Momma opened the door and I hugged her as tight as I could. Instantly, I knew that everything would be alright. Mom showed me around the apartment; it was gorgeous. Mom accommodated the extra bedroom to my liking. She placed fresh towels, linen, and a pillow on the couch. Mom and Stacy struggled to get acclimated to a new lifestyle. The emotional and financial detachments were their biggest challenges; but I was there to help. I told mom and Stacy all about Boston and the NFL. However, mom appeared more concerned about my health. She asked me was I still praying; I smiled and answered yes!

Daddy was my biggest ambassador. He must have taken me to every house in the neighborhood, showing me off and talking about his trip to Boston. He told neighbors how I ran the kick-off's back. He was a proud father. Dad reached for the keys to the BMW and drove the car around with the music blasting. I was his trophy and that was his moment of fame. I wished that I could have bought dad a BMW too. It was gratifying to discover that J was in great health and spirits. She was 88 years old and hanging on to life the best she could; she had the ultimate will to survive.

Jack and I started where we left off, acting silly. We were eager to hit the town. It was nice visiting with old friends around the neighborhood. I was just as happy to see them as they were to see me. I never wanted them to feel that I had forgotten about them. I decided to go back to my high school, Ribault. I became a substitute teacher for one month. That was my way of giving back to my community. Some mornings it was really rough finding the strength to get up at 6AM. I was exactly what the students needed, a role model. They were intrigued by my presence. I shared my experiences with them and answered questions about the NFL. It didn't take long before the word had spread over campus. Many students tried to skip their classes to come hear me speak. I was honored, but they were swiftly sent back to class. Instead, the school invited me to speak at a rally.

Playing in the NFL exposed me to prominent dignitaries, and I participated in many celebrity functions. Slowly, I was matriculating among the upper echelon of society, but I preserved my humility and never abandoned my roots.

By now it was February and I had a lot to accomplish before mini-camp. It was imperative for me to go to Orlando and help Renita plan our wedding. We decided to get married July 2, a couple of weeks before training camp. Also, I registered for summer classes at UCF. I had a treacherous schedule. Focusing on school, a wedding, and football was exhausting; but getting my degree was important.

However, it was displeasing leaving J. She adored having me around; I hadn't seen her that happy in years. J told everyone that her grandson played pro-football; she was extremely proud. I autographed a team picture and hung it over her bed. Meanwhile, dad and I spent time fishing. We dreamt about getting a boat one day and going where the big fish were. The Welfare Bridge was a popular fishing location for poor folks; thus earning its name. Hundreds of anglers baited their hooks and hoped to catch a meal; nothing was thrown back into the water. We fried the smaller fish crispy and ate the bones and all. Many of the people there were my fans; we talked more about football than fishing. They were genuine good people that would have given you the shirt off their backs.

The next week, I helped mom find another car. She never told me how dangerous her car was. Mom was stopping her old Chevy Chevette with the emergency brake. That broke my heart, so we went car shopping every night until we came across a good deal and a car mom liked. She wasn't very picky and would have taken anything, that's how humble she was. I couldn't afford a lot, especially with a wedding approaching. Nevertheless, we found the cutest little car, a blue Pontiac Sun Bird with a sunroof; mom was happy.

The following week I relocated to Orlando. I was 22 years old and entering my second year into the NFL. I had served my community and shared quality time with my family and loved ones. Now, I was embarking on a college degree, and engaged to marry the woman I loved. I was really content and felt proud of my accomplishments. Renita and I lived in a two bedroom apartment three miles from campus. Renita worked while I attended class. It was very important to stay in good shape because Coach Kyatt, our defensive line coach, was scheduled to visit me in two weeks to administer conditioning drills. I didn't take it seriously and made every excuse not to practice. I had gotten lazy and fallen behind in my school work. That wasn't a good sign if I planned on graduating. But I had bitten off too much to swallow, and something had to give. I was embarrassed with my performance and I ensured Coach Kyatt better results in camp. I agonized over how Coach Berry would receive the news. I decided to drop out of school and dedicate the remaining time training for the upcoming season. I practiced with a chip on my shoulder. That was just the spark I needed because I vowed to never be caught unprepared again, especially with something as important as my career.

However, contrary to sound judgment, Renita and I purchased a puppy; he was the cutest thing. Zeus was a Rottweiler; he was the runt of the litter. I walked him with pride, as scores of admirers raved over his beauty. Zeus was a frisky fellow. Constantly, he demanded our attention, especially during teething. He delighted in me rubbing his gums, but occasionally he preferred biting my toes. Those sharp little teeth went through anything.

My neighbor couldn't resist playing with Zeus. He used to kneel down and grab him by the snout and say, "You miss your mommy? You miss your mommy?"

Zeus barked, wagged his tail, and licked him all over his face. I don't know who enjoyed it most, Zeus or my neighbor. Nevertheless, potty training Zeus was a nightmare. He preferred going inside rather than outside.

Tony Collins was waived from the Patriots for violating the NFL substance abuse policy. I was disturbed by the news, but it was a great opportunity, because I had one less running back to compete against. The starting position was open for competition, and I was a serious contender. Unexpectedly, the Patriots drafted two running backs, John Stephens and Marvin Allen. I was discouraged, but I understood it was business, and not personal. I took it as a challenge, so I worked a lot harder and a lot smarter.

The wedding was approaching at an accelerated pace and we needed to make a decision about the ceremony; we chose to have a church wedding in our home town. Besides choosing my best man and my groomsmen, I left the details to Renita and her mom. I needed to concentrate on training.

With the draft over, I flew into Boston for mini-camp. It was nice seeing my teammates; they greeted me vivaciously. My confidence soared high; I expected to have a stellar year. I battled with Reggie Dupard for the starting running back position. The odds were clearly in my favor. Reggie was a former number one pick, but he was under accomplished. My emergence evoked trade rumors and the battle became fierce. However, I was in the perfect position to become the next starting running back for the New England Patriots. I had a great camp, the coaches marveled over my acrobatic moves. Luckily, I didn't sustain any injuries. My roommate was a bruising full back out of Brigham Young. Bruce Hansen and I became great friends; we shared many philosophical and religious opinions. After minicamp, we enjoyed feasting on Maine lobster in our hotel suite; the taste was delectable.

I extended my stay in Foxboro and played on our off-season basketball team; it was a great way to keep in shape and earn extra money. We traveled throughout the northeast playing as many as six games a week; we had an arduous schedule. However, I was vindicated by the loyal fans that attended in droves our best player was Cedric Jones; he was a polished performer. Some of the games were quite competitive, but we always prevailed.

When I returned home from minicamp, Renita and I left Orlando and moved in with momma to put the final touches on the wedding. On July 2, 1988 I married Renita in the First Baptist Church of Oakland. It was a beautiful ceremony. The church décor was gray and peach, and seven candles burned on each side of the altar. The pews were filled to capacity and everyone sat nervously anticipating the bride's appearance. I waited patiently at the altar with Jack at my side. Suddenly, the pianist played the wedding march; the audience arose.

The palms of my hands began sweating and my mouth felt parched. I was terrified, but the moment I laid eyes on Renita my fears subsided and a smile resonated on my face. Renita's wedding dress complimented her beauty; she appeared as an angel. Slowly, she walked towards the altar with her father to join me. Immediately, Jack reached into his pocket and retrieved the ring. Renita's hand trembled as I place the ring on her finger. We gazed into each other's eyes and repeated our vows. After kissing my bride we were pronounced man and wife. I felt a presence from within that went beyond words; it was a divine experience.

However, we postponed our honeymoon and prepared to drive to Boston before training camp. Early the next morning I loaded the

BMW with our suitcases and wedding gifts; mom prepared snacks for the road. She made sure we didn't leave anything behind. Somehow I built up the nerves to say goodbye, it was very emotional.

My new wife and I walked out that front door to start our new life. Only God knew our destiny, but many prayers left with us that day. We hugged our loved ones and got into the car. Momma and daddy stood expressionless, they appeared sad. I took a deep breath and cranked the engine I had apprehensions and considered staying another night, but courageously I put the car in gear and drove away. I watched my momma and Stacy from the rearview mirror. They didn't move an inch. They stood and watched as I faded out of view. I felt guilty leaving mom and Stacy behind, they had nothing and I was going off to live the good life with my wife I wish I could have taken them with me. Many times I wanted to turn around and go back for one last hug, but I had to be strong and secure a future for my wife.

The tears dripped from my eyes much faster than Renita could wipe away. Nothing she did or said could stop them from falling. I cried until I reached Savannah, Georgia; it was the saddest day of my life.

Renita said, "It'll be alright. Your mom will be just fine."

No one understood my pain, it required divine intervention. I played a gospel song to settle my soul. Amazingly, my spirit responded.

Renita and I sang gospel music and I prayed aloud. I didn't think it was possible to smile again, but I did. God had restored my soul. I called mom on my cell phone and told her that I loved her. However, the emotional stress had made me fatigue.

We stopped in a rest area to sleep and use the restroom. Zeus appeared distracted; he didn't relieve himself. Shortly, Renita took the wheel and headed north. Zeus enjoyed the ride; he sat on the floor under my legs and slept. When I woke up we were near Washington D.C. I figured we had had enough driving for one day, we needed to find a hotel that accepted pets; we didn't have any luck.

Our persistence was rewarded; we found a Best Western near the Landover Mall in Maryland. We were ahead of schedule, with plenty of time before the start of camp. But it made perfect sense to get there early in order to find a place to live. Renita and I left Zeus in the hotel and went joy riding. I had never seen so many black people in all of my life. Now, I realized why D.C. is called the Chocolate City. It was beautiful seeing black people in unity because where I'm from black people were destroying the community and each other. We even rode by the Washington Monument. We had a great time in Washington, but it was time to go.

Ironically, we decided to stay over in New York. New York was mammoth; the buildings loomed larger than life. I was mesmerized!

Downtown was congested and motorists drove recklessly. I made sure to look twice and be extra careful. Driving was difficult, and so was finding a hotel that accepted pets. We had no choice but to keep on driving.

Our next stop was Philadelphia and again the answer was, "I'm sorry we don't accept pets."

Renita and I took a break; we were exhausted. Zeus was also getting frazzled; we fed him and took him for a long walk. No matter how much food he consumed, he never relieved himself; I was concerned. Either something was wrong, or he was just going to explode with poop all over my car. We tried waiting on Zeus as long as we could before driving off. I expected him to drop a load, instead he passed gas. But Zeus only passed a little gas. It smelled awful, but if it was good enough for him it was good enough for me. Sparks would soon turn into flames.

I drove throughout the night until we reached Rhode Island. By now, we didn't care if they accepted pets or not. Zeus was going inside somebody's hotel room. We craved a hot shower and a comfortable bed. A hotel with a lobby entrance would be disastrous; we had to sneak Zeus in inconspicuously. Luckily, we found a motel with rooms on the outside. We took a risk and hoped that Zeus wouldn't bark. Our scheme appeared to work, we had retired for the night. Suddenly, Zeus howled like a wolf; there must have been a full moon. We packed our bags and anticipated a knock on the door. Somehow, we survived the night without any complaints. The next morning Renita and I went out for breakfast, but Zeus remained behind. I turned up the volume on the TV and placed the "do not disturb" sign on the door. When we returned, the maids were standing by our door; I knew something was wrong.

Housekeeping approached me and said, "We know that you have a dog inside, he's been barking ever since you left. But don't worry, we won't tell." Finally, we could rest and set our minds at ease. I cleaned up the pee and crap that Zeus left on the floor; he had exploded. I guess when he had to go, he had to go.

With only a few miles before Foxboro my only concern was finding a place for us until training camp. This time, we were lucky because we found a Best Western that accepted Zeus and it wasn't far away from camp. After checking in with Bobby Grier, I was all about business. In between workouts, I looked for a realtor. It was essential to find a house before camp, but it demanded time. I feared leaving Renita with too much responsibility. Luckily, one of my teammates gave me the name of a realtor. Luke was an experienced realtor from Franklin, MA; we adored him. He was really funny and seemed to have our best interest at heart. Luke referred us to a new development site in Cumberland,

RI. It was on a ski resort that had been converted into condos. Eagerly, we made an appointment to see the model.

Luke chauffeured us in his SUV; it was an adventurous journey that took us through rolling hills with a panoramic view of the country side. Diamond Hill was an oasis nestled perfectly in paradise; it was heaven on earth. Luke entertained us in a three bedroom condo on a corner lot; it was huge! My favorite was the basement and the Jacuzzi in the master suite; it felt like home, but another prospect had already made an offer. Luke suggested that we fill out the paperwork just in case the other family was denied. We followed his advice and hoped for the best.

Meanwhile, camp was only one week away and our options were limited. I pestered Luke daily, but was denied an answer. After returning from lunch, we received a call; it was Luke. I walked out and paced on the balcony; the drama was so intense. Minutes later, Renita joined me; she was calm and collective. Suddenly, she laminated with joy and screamed, "We got it! We got it!"

It was great news and it couldn't have come at a better time. That same day we said goodbye to the Best Western and picked up our key from Luke, and then moved into our brand new place.

Shopping for furniture was time consuming; I delegated the responsibility to Renita. I had to prepare for camp and secure our future.

Ed and his family were thrilled to have us as his neighbors; he and his wife were both professors. With their help, we became acquainted with our environment. However, without furniture and appliances we lived a modest lifestyle. During the day we ate fast food, at night we made a pallet and slept on the floor. Our sleep was erupted with exotic sounds deep within the forest. But Zeus and I patrolled the premises, guarding against any wood-be intruders.

Finally, training camp had arrived, and my time with Renita had come to a crescendo. I was extremely nervous; I ate a light breakfast to settle my stomach. After prayer, Renita drove me to Bryant College in Smithfield, RI. I barely said a word; I was locked into a zone. Renita respected my privacy, and she focused on the road. It didn't take long to arrive, I knew a shortcut. After I checked into camp, Renita and I sat outside under an apple tree until curfew. Our close proximity to camp didn't make saying goodbye any easier.

Many perks came along with being a veteran. I didn't have to climb stairs, my room was conveniently located on the first floor; it simplified moving and it came in handy during stressful workouts. The most popular conversation in camp was centered around our top draft choice. John Stephens was unsigned and his demands were unresolved. For selfish reasons, I considered it a blessing. Nevertheless, I breezed through conditioning drills; I was in peak shape. Clearly, I was the most impressive athlete at my position, if not on the team. It was important for me to be a leader and set the tempo; so far the mission was accomplished.

Our first team meeting was dynamic. Coach Berry challenged the team to work relentlessly and recapture the AFC championship; we responded to the message with a jarring applause. But, the milder temperatures were elusive, and a lower jet stream hoyed blistering heat into New England. Quickly, the weather took its toll and restricted many players from participating in drills. I drank plenty of water to remain hydrated. My goal was to survive camp without sustaining an injury.

Contrary to my rookie season, I was fashioned to play a prominent role on offense. Also, I was considered a viable weapon on the kickoff return team. I felt optimistic about my future with the Patriots, even with John Stephens arrival. John was a punishing runner; he attacked the defense with a vengeance. But, his upright running style jeopardized his longevity, and his body absorbed tenacious blows. However, my strength was speed and elusiveness. In addition to John Stephens, the Patriots acquired Doug Flutie. He was a local legend and the 1984 Heisman Trophy winner; Bostonians loved him. Doug was one of the nicest guys I had ever met. He couldn't have been much taller than 5'8" but he played like a giant. He recalled meeting me at UCF when he played for the New Jersey Generals. I was honored to have him as a teammate; he was everybody's All-American hero. The players felt that we had the final ingredient to return to the Super Bowl. Practice was intense. With a talented roster, no position was secure.

The big scrimmage against the Redskins in Carlisle, Pennsylvania was only a week away. I had a phenomenal week of practice. Bobby Grier promoted me into the starting lineup against the Redskin's; my performance was impressive. After the game, I chatted with some of the NFL legends. Charles Mann, Dexter Manley, Wilber Marshall, Darryl Green, and Art Monk were ambassadors of the game, and both teams demonstrated the utmost respect for each other on and off the field.

Each day I made progress. The offensive and defensive schemes were beginning to register, and I was playing proactive instead of reactive. It was all coming together, until that dreadful day that changed the course of my life. It was a wet and muggy afternoon as light showers moved through Smithfield, Rhode Island. We had just finished 7 on 7 and it was time for the offensive and defensive teams to scrimmage when Bobby called my name. I was surprised that he called me to scrimmage with the first team, but I was ready. It was a special play designed just for me. Everything was perfect. I caught the ball and accelerated around the end with a blocker in front. There it was, a gaping hole. My only challenge was getting through it before it closed.

I planted my foot and made a sharp cut as hard and as fast as I could. Suddenly, I heard a loud sound; it came from my hamstring. The pain rendered me helpless, it was impossible to run. I threw the football into the ground with rage, and hopped off the field screaming "fuck." I knew that it was bad, real bad. Coach Berry stopped practice. My teammates and coaches gathered around and shook their heads, but no one felt worse than me. Ron O'Neil wrapped my leg with an ice bag and carted me off the field toward the training room. Every bump and turn that he made while driving sent chills and sharp pain up my leg. I felt a strong, throbbing sensation in my hamstring that resembled a heartbeat. Before we reached the training room, my hamstring had begun swelling. With Ron's assistance, I hopped gingerly up each stair until I reached the training room. Trying to explain what had happened was just as painful as my injury. My dreams were drenched in sorrow, and my heart was shattered. Immediately, I began treatment and started the arduous road to recovery.

Shortly afterward, Bobby Grier came in and asked about my injury. I was diagnosed with a pulled hamstring. Only time could determine the extent of my injury. I missed the beginning of preseason two consecutive years. My injury allowed others an opportunity to make the team. My career was in great jeopardy. As a result, I lived in constant fear and anxiety of being cut. I began to worry. I sought Bobby Grier for consultation, but he couldn't promise me a roster spot.

Bobby looked at me and sternly said, "I'm concerned!"

I prepared for the worst and hoped for the best.

Sleeping at night was agonizing; no position seemed comfortable. I prayed and listened to gospel music, hoping to steal a peaceful night's sleep. Some nights, I talked with Renita. She offered comforting words and Bible scriptures for me to read. On Sundays I went home, it was my day off; however, my visitations were abbreviated. Being late for mandatory treatment resulted in a huge fine.

As a full time spectator, I had plenty of time to observe some of the other players. There was one player in particular, a talented little wide receiver from the University of Illinois. He had blazing speed and the grace of a Gazelle. There was something very unique about him as a player and as a person. He was small in stature, but fearless. Darryl Usher was funny, entertaining, and extremely spiritual. He was the number one kick returner in the Big 10 and second overall in the nation. Darryl earned All American recognition and the University of Illinois most valuable player. I watched him run routes and return kickoffs to perfection; he was astonishing! During breaks I bragged about his craftsmanship. He was extremely humble, and his attitude was sublime. I became his biggest fan. However, preseason cuts were days away; it would take a miracle for Darryl to survive. He had a better chance of winning the lottery! I offered him my prayers and friendship. Darryl was very apprehensive, and he clung to my side.

Most of my teammates played out of desperation or fear. The thought of getting cut plagued our minds, and the incentive of making an NFL roster outweighed any health risk. A vast majority of players gambled and took calculated risks to become rich and famous; but odds were clearly against them. Hordes of players departed from the game dishonored, sustaining both physical and psychological damage; I found myself in the same predicament. However, my saving grace was speed and agility.

After practice, Darryl rushed over to me and asked, "How did I do?"

He valued my opinion. Many circumstances prohibited us from conversing, but we had a special language. Sometimes it only took a smile or a slap on the buttocks; he knew exactly what it meant. We approached our first preseason game, and Foxboro Stadium was filled to capacity. Darryl suffered from pregame jitters, but I remained close to his side. Constantly, I reminded him that God was with him.

I watched him from the sidelines as he warmed up and went through drills. I stared into his eyes and nodded my head. I would have given anything to be on that field with him. Darryl was used mostly as a punt returner on special teams. All was going well until Darryl limped off the field. He gripped his knee and whist in agonizing pain. Immediately, I knew that something was terribly wrong.

Darryl came to me and said, "My knee feels funny, my knee!"

The next time I saw Darryl, he was sitting on the bench with an ice bag on his knee. He was a spectator just like me. I felt his pain, and I tried to comfort him, but it was to no avail. Darryl needed more than words. That was his last preseason game. He was diagnosed with a ligament strain that could possibly require surgery. It was the worst news any player could receive.

Darryl and I spent countless hours rehabilitating together. We hoped for another chance to play before it was too late. Unfortunately, Darryl and I forfeited our entire preseason. Our injuries were much worse than predicted. Nevertheless, we formed an inseparable bond that changed our lives. I took him everywhere, including home on the weekends. He struggled getting around on his crutches, but I was there to help.

Darryl cherished my BMW; he pledged to buy one just like it. We drove to my home in Cumberland. Darryl was happy to see me doing well. I was convinced that he was genuine and it came from his heart. Moments later, Renita entered the room. Darryl was startled, he wasn't expecting her. He attempted to stand with his crutches to honor her presence, but Renita insisted that he remain seated.

Darryl was extremely polite. Often, he'd respond by saying, "yes ma'am." He even referred to Renita as Mrs. Davis.

She'd smile and say, "Just call me Renita."

His meekness made an indelible impression, and that day Darryl became a part of our family.

Darryl really missed his family, especially his girlfriend, Mimi. He talked about her constantly and expressed his plans to make her his wife. But no one meant as much to Darryl as his mom. Alma lived in California, and she was the treasure of his heart. Darryl wanted to relocate her to Boston, but first he needed to make the team. Having a bum knee severely diminished his chances, but he got lucky. Darryl landed a spot on the injury reserve. That was great news; he was secured a weekly paycheck. My team status had also been determined. My injury was a major handicap and it landed my sophomore campaign on the injury reserve list. I was disappointed. My goals exceeded the norm, and I considered the injury reserve as a failure.

It was painful watching my career deteriorate. Darryl and I regurgitated our feelings to one another, and acknowledged our spiritual deprivation. We attended Bible Study for prayer and guidance. I needed God more than ever; I was under a severe trial. Darryl immediately received his blessing; he purchased his dream car, a BMW. Soon, Mimi moved in with him; they were a cute couple.

Instantly, the girls bonded and became friends. Darryl and I reverend our cars; it signified our success. We profiled around town with the music blasting to our favorite group, EPMD (Eric and Parrish Making Dollars). Back then life was fun; we were young and successful. Often, we were profiled and harassed without a cause; especially while driving in the black communities. Racism was a thriving factor in Boston, and playing with the Patriots didn't minimize its effects.

I enjoyed double dating; I felt like a teenager. The girls loved going to concerts; Luther Vandross and Anita Baker were the best. Shortly after, Darryl's mother flew into Boston; it was nice to see them together. It did my heart good. Darryl was elated; he had his two favorite women in town. Ms. Usher was much taller than I expected; he must have gotten his height from his father's side of the family. Nevertheless, she was very sweet and kind. I could certainly tell where Darryl got his charm from; he was a chip off the block!

Being on injury reserve didn't ensure any stability on the team. I was considered a liability and lived in fear. My hamstring responded poorly to treatment; it tormented me. The slightest movement triggered pain, and I took circumstances into my own hands. Mosi Tatupu offered me a healing crystal. It was about the size of a quarter. Mosi demonstrated its unusual characteristics by tying it onto a string and placing it inches over my hand. The crystal rotated clockwise, and then he positioned it over my injury. Amazingly, the crystal changed directions and rotated counter clockwise. It had a mind of its own. Instantly, I felt a warm tingling sensation. It was strange. Mosi ensured me that it would heal my hamstring. His conviction encouraged me, and my faith was rejuvenated. I never left home without the crystal. Each night I filled my tub with warm water and Epson Salt and immersed until I became drowsy.

Renita tried her best to console me. Frequently, I'd open the Bible to the 23rd chapter of Psalms and wrap it around my hamstring with an ace bandage. I relied on the word of God; if he couldn't help, no one could. I had convinced myself that my condition would improve overnight, but I was gravely mistaken. When morning arrived, my wishful thinking came to an abrupt end. The pages of my Bible were dismantled and my problematic injury lingered on.

Subsequently, Ron O'Neil scheduled me an appointment with the team physician. Dr. Zarins thoroughly examined my injury. I laid on my stomach with both legs extending forward. Suddenly, Dr. Zarins placed both hands around my ankle and demanded me to bend my leg backwards towards my buttocks. As I attempted, he pressed forward. I experienced an acute pain in my hamstring. Then, he forced his finger against my hamstring. I reached for Ron's hand and gripped it firmly until the pain subsided. Dr. Zarins prepared to administer another Cortisone shot. However, the examination aggravated my hamstring and made the problematic area impossible to identify. As a consequence, I received multiple injections of Cortisone. I wasn't keen on getting shots, but I took a calculated risk. I was under tremendous pressure to reclaim my career. I was totally oblivious to the risk of taking Cortisone. From my vantage point, it gave me the best chance of getting back on the field and saving my career. I had come too far to turn back; I was trapped. After all, it was a common practice among the players on our team.

Meanwhile, Darryl later received great news. The doctor was convinced that he had improved enough to participate in practice; he was elated. Within days the Cortisone had alleviated my symptoms, and I was allowed to weight train and jog.

In early November, New England was absolutely beautiful. A litany of colors adorned the hills. Zeus and I often hiked down the mountain trail to a secluded lake. The ebony water glistened as sunrays beamed from above. Flocks of Canadian Geese flew over head; it was a picture made for heaven. Zeus and I were accepted by nature and roamed freely. He'd often disappear in the forest. I'd shout out his name and the sound of my voice reverberated. Zeus returned panting with his tongue hanging out. Gently, I rubbed his head. He demonstrated his affection by licking my face and wagging his tail. Quickly, he wandered to the shore and lapped up a drink of cold water. My favorite was throwing rocks and making them ricochet on top of the water; sometimes they triple skipped. My problems vanished when I remembered how to be a kid. Its tranquil effect was the perfect anecdote.

On other occasions, Zeus and I jogged up the mountain. Smoke seeped from our mouths, while we jumped over rocks and rotten logs. Autumn foliage sprinkled from the tree tops and camouflaged the surface. I felt God's presence and he spoke to me in a unique language. On the summit, I glanced across the valley and reflected on my incredible journey. I felt a insatiable need to pray and make peace with God. However, I was confronted with turmoil, and I didn't know which direction to turn in life. But, I didn't have a problem asking God for help; I was confident that he wouldn't abandon me, and I accepted each trial as an opportunity to grow spiritually. It reminded me of a story: There once was a donkey that fell into a ditch and no one would help him. By passers threw stones at the donkey until the ditch filled up and the donkey was able to walk right out of the ditch. The moral of the story is, every knock is a boost. That was the story of my life because the more I got knocked down, the more I got up. My attitude determined my altitude.

When I look back at my trials and tribulations, they certainly made me stronger and a more compassionate person. I often thought about my journey and to this day I still wonder how I made it. Unlike so many players, I never had great stats or records. Heck, I never rushed for over 1000 yards in one season, yet I made it to the NFL. It was a long and rigorous journey, but I made it.

It wasn't easy growing up. My parents' divorce was an emotional challenge. At times, dad's alcohol abuse made living unbearable. However, college was a cultivating experience, though initially I struggled. It was a miracle being drafted into the NFL from an unknown school, and staying healthy was next to impossible. The vicissitudes of life were a heavy burden; but, it was obvious that God was carrying me on his shoulders. Many others were worthy of standing in place, but God chose me for a unique purpose. I realized that I had a lot to be thankful for, and that God was preparing me for a blessing. Each dissention was designed for ascension; but, the quality of my faith was crucial in determining the outcome. I returned home with a new perspective.

Darryl and I remained in Rhode Island while the team traveled. We both swallowed our pride and prepared ourselves mentally by analyzing our playbook. Soon, I made enough progress to start practicing with the team. I felt like a rookie all over again; it was my first time back on the field in over a month, but I was eager to make my presence known. I wore a thigh sleeve to prevent another tear, and Darryl wore a bulky knee brace. Each day we made more and more progress, until finally, the knee brace and thigh sleeve came off. Darryl and I stayed in arms reach of each other during practice; we were inseparable. The team referred to us as Frick and Frack. I never quite understood what it meant, but we both responded in a positive way.

Darryl and I were instrumental players on the scout team, but our ultimate goal was making the active roster. We practiced with a passion to excel; it was the only chance we had to display our talent. Before practice, we caught at least a hundred passes or more. During practice, we simulated the opposing team's offense. We took our role seriously. After making spectacular catches, Darryl returned to the huddle gasping for air. Often, he'd spit and blow his nose to clear the mucus. When Darryl wasn't catching passes, I was dazzling spectators with arm breaking tackles for long runs.

After practice, we returned punt and kick-offs; we were among the last two to leave the stadium. We were dedicated. Our mission was to become the best running back and wide receiver tandem in the entire National Football League. Nothing was going to stop us, I mean nothing! We ended each day by sitting in the hot and cold whirlpools, followed by a deep tissue massage. We anticipated being rewarded for our hard work and dedication; it didn't take long. My break came the next week when Marvin Allen was lost for the season with a fractured shoulder. Darryl filled the last spot as a result of another injury. We were both back in action as members of the active roster; our dream had come true. Renita and Mimi were extremely proud. My first game was against the Miami Dolphins.

Darryl and I drove our BMW's to the stadium and crammed into the team bus. It was a cold dreary day. Snow showers were predicted in the immediate forecast. Darryl and I secured our vehicles with car covers before leaving Foxboro Stadium. Some of the players thought we were odd and began mocking us.

Nevertheless, it was great playing in Miami. The weather was perfect. It was ideal for my hamstring; I was eager to play. Neither Darryl nor I contributed much, but it sure felt great dressing out and being on the field with my teammates. After the game I reunited on the field with a former teammate. Tony Franklin had missed a game winning field goal, and he departed the stadium with his head held low.

We returned to Boston in the remnants of a blizzard; it was a dismal contrast to Miami. The BMW's were submerged in snow. Foxboro resembled a ghost town. Darryl and I had the last laugh; we saw the same guys that mocked us scraping snow off of their windshields.

It was extremely difficult driving in the snow. We got three inches of snow. It was time for a change. I went to the Ford dealership across from the stadium to buy a truck. There were so many to choose, and I didn't have a clue where to start. I figured that I needed a four wheel drive. The salesman recognized me and I gave him an autograph. He tried to sell me a new truck. But I had no intention on spending a lot of money. I wanted something simple, that's it! Then, he showed me the prefect truck; a Ford Bronco. I didn't have to look twice; I was sold. This time I had no problem getting financed. I had enough to buy it cash. And it was just in time because more snow was in the forecast.

Throughout the week, my hamstring continued to improve and I had made the active roster two consecutive weeks; this time our opponent was the Indianapolis Colts. I was used primarily as a return specialist. The dome was extremely noisy. The fans stood on their feet and cheered when Eric Dickerson touched the ball; he was a dynamic football player. Our defense quickly silenced the crowd, and limited Eric Dickerson to a mediocre performance. It's suffice to say that our special teams gave us a tremendous boost.

On our first possession, we returned the kick-off for a touchdown. Sammy and I stood near the end zone waiting to receive the kick; we

were a deadly combination. It was a high swirling kick that landed into Sammy's arms. Quickly, I led him through a gaping hole along the left side, and Sammy did the rest. He took it all the way for the longest run of the year. I joined Sammy in the end zone for a touchdown celebration. Once the adrenaline had worn off, I felt a piercing pain in my leg. I tweaked my hamstring, but I vowed to keep it a secret. I found myself in big trouble. I had to adjust the game to my discomfort. My performance was greatly diminished, and I barely displayed a glimpse of my ability. It was disheartening and I was mentally distraught.

When I returned to Foxboro I received another dose of Cortisone. This time it was oral. I took several pills over a seven day span. My body didn't respond the way I had expected, but I continued practicing as if nothing was wrong.

Soon, I had something to cheer about; the holiday's had arrived and we were expecting guests. It was Renita's first time preparing Thanksgiving dinner. She was extremely nervous and relied on Mimi's help. But, Mimi couldn't cook; Renita was traumatized. Darryl and I were in serious trouble. The girls plundered around in the kitchen looking for pots and pans to cook the turkey and collard greens in. Darryl and I entertained ourselves with a six-pack. Soon, the smell of food was in the air; I was starved.

The table setting was beautiful, neatly decorated with our finest china. It was filled with all of the Thanksgiving treats that we loved. I was very proud of the girls. Darryl and I piled our plates with food. Then, we bowed our heads and said grace. The girls watched tentatively as Darryl bit into the turkey. Suddenly, Darryl stopped chewing and frowned; something was wrong. Bluntly he said, "This turkey tastes horrible. I think it's raw. I wish momma was here to cook!"

The room was silent; we stared at Darryl with our mouths wide open. Mimi reprimanded Darryl's repulsive comment; she demanded an apology. Renita smiled and accepted his apology, and we resumed eating. Later, Darryl atoned for his remarks and washed dishes. The loving memories of our first Thanksgiving made it a day to remember forever.

We were midway through the season when the Seattle Seahawks came into town, and I invited dad and Emma to come. They arrived in Boston on the Peter Pan Bus. Scores of people loitered in front of the bus terminal; it was the busiest travel season of the year. My heart was afflicted seeing the homeless lay motionless on the icy sidewalk, but I fought through my emotions and held onto my wallet as I made my way towards the terminal. I searched for the biggest smile; I knew that it would be daddy. He was dressed in a red and blue sweat suit; he and Emma looked fantastic. I was relieved to see him sober. Swiftly, I made my way across the lobby and cradled them into my arms. We were engaged momentarily in frivolous dialogue. Soon, I grabbed their luggage, and we scurried out and ate dinner at my favorite Restaurant, No Name.

Shortly after we arrived home, the doorbell rang. I peeped out of the window and recognized Darryl. Daddy was anxious to meet him; he accompanied me to the door. I opened the door and Darryl greeted us with a warm smile. Before I had an opportunity to introduce them to one another, Darryl shouted, dad! Immediately, dad reciprocated and shouted, Darryl! Then, they cuddled into each other's arms. Darryl made an everlasting impact on their hearts. Dad and Emma adored him; they were saddened to see him depart. Daddy and Emma enjoyed their visit. Renita entertained them in Boston while I prepared for the

Seattle Seahawks. I thought about dad during practice; I was eager to get home. But my arrival was detained; I was subjected to mandatory treatment. Nevertheless, we made it to dinner on time. We ended our day at the movies; <u>Coming to America</u> was hilarious! Dad and Emma laughed hysterically, and I rejoiced over their happiness. Giving and receiving love from my family enriched my heart; I was extremely proud. During dad and Emma's leisure time they walked with Zeus down the mountain; it was physically debilitating, and demanded peak stamina. Dad and Emma returned out of breath, and prepared for bed; they were exhausted. However, they anxiously anticipated kickoff. The big game was rapidly approaching; it was less than twenty-four hours away. I secluded myself and meditated in the jacuzzi for therapy.

On game day, I arrived at the stadium hours before kickoff to receive treatment. It was much too early for them to leave with me, so they remained behind. Carefully, I bundled up in my winter gear and kissed my family goodbye. After the game, I congregated with my family in the players lobby. It was a joyous moment; we defeated the Seahawks 13-7. Our fans and guests cordially greeted one another. Dad met and took pictures with several players; his favorite was Doug Flutie. Dad was like a fish in water, he never met a stranger. A fan even invited us to go fishing at his home in Rhode Island. It was a Tuesday morning, and the weather was perfect for fishing. Dad stopped for coffee along the way; he couldn't do without. Slowly, I drove around the winding country roads, searching for his address. Dad sat in the passenger seat and sipped hot coffee. We bypassed glamorous homes; most of them were camouflaged by majestic trees. The scenery was breathtaking. Soon, we arrived at our destination; his home was nestled in a shaded nook. John greeted us in the driveway and welcomed us into his home. He was grateful for our coming, and serenaded us with a delicious breakfast. Unfortunately, he couldn't join us; his presence was requested back at the office. John apologized and told us to make ourselves at home. He had prepared for our arrival, and supplied his home to meet our accommodations. John escorted us outside to his sanctuary. We were enthralled by a sunken glass lake surrounded by mountains. There were endless views of beauty. The shadows from the clouds above pranced on top of the water.

Then, he unveiled his boat and threw me the keys and said, "The tank is full and there's plenty of food in the fridge. Have fun!"

We toured the lake searching for Brim and Bass. Finally, we located a favorable spot near a patch of lily pads. It was ideal for big mouth Bass. We hooked a fish on nearly every cast. Soon, the sun had abandoned its post and swarming critters chased us onto the shore. Dad, Emma, and I shared a day in heaven, and I treasured every moment. It was memories like that that made saying goodbye the next day difficult.

The following week, the Tampa Bay Buccaneers arrived in town, and playoff implications were at stake; each player's future lied in the ballot. The team's morale was greatly intensified, and we practiced with a sense of urgency. But, my chronic injury handicapped my performance. Darryl and I sat in the whirlpool and encouraged one another. However, a grim reality came to mind; Darryl and I were in the final year of our contract, and losing him as a teammate made me extremely mournful. Unless we resigned with the Patriots, which was highly unlikely, we were free to shop the market for more money. Our future with the Patriots looked bleak; injuries raised overwhelming doubt. It appeared that we'd become a business casualty. Suddenly, it made sense why everybody started practicing harder. They were fighting to get resigned for more money, and a good week of practice could reduce the chances of the team drafting a replacement. I found myself in the middle of a political warfare and all weapons were aimed at me. I needed to get healthy and record a stunning performance; but, chances of both happening were slim to none. Darryl and I were in trouble, the handwriting was on the wall. We prepared for the worst but hoped for the best.

With another win under our belt against Tampa, we were only one game away from making the playoffs. But first, we had to go on the road and face a hostile crowd at Mile High Stadium. The Denver

Broncos were highly respected and auditioned the games most prolific passers. John Elway was a fierce competitor that terrorized opposing defenses. But Coach Berry orchestrated a brilliant game plan that was designed to lasso the Broncos. The media broadcasted a live interview in front of Sullivan Stadium while zealous fans rallied outside to show their support.

Our trip to Denver was tedious; Darryl and I slept most of the way. Some of my teammates entertained themselves over a friendly game of chess. Once we arrived in Denver, I found myself wandering downtown treading through the mud and snow that doused the city. I was captivated over the carolers; they warmed the heats of pedestrians with their Christmas spirits. As I walked towards the hotel, I stood in obeisance and marveled at the beauty of the Rocky Mountains. After dinner, I completed my pre-game ritual before bed. I soaked in a tub of hot water to relax and loosen my hamstring. Periodically, I added more hot water; it felt like a steam room. The mirror fogged and sweat beads rolled down my face. Soon, I felt the signs of fatigue and thirst. Before finding my way to bed, I drank cold water from the melted ice that sat in the hotel's ice bucket. Then I stretched my hamstring for the big game. That was something I did before each game and Denver was no exception.

The next morning, I boarded the bus to play the most important game of my career. Mile High Stadium was drenched in tradition, and boisterous fans made their presence known. However, we emerged from the locker room in solidarity, and commenced to perform our pregame drills. Within minutes we began hyperventilating; the stadium was a mile above sea level. My teammates and I gasped for air. Suddenly, there was a look of desperation. Then I heard a loud roar, as John Elway led the Broncos onto the field; the crowd went wild! The Broncos were ill affected by the altitude; I knew that we were in for a long night.

Our game plan was simple; pressure John Elway and prevent him from making big plays outside of the pocket. We executed our strategy to perfection, and led going into half time. We entered the locker room in complete silence. It wasn't a time to celebrate; the battle had just begun. Before taking the field, coach reminded us not to give up any big plays.

On the first series, Irvin Fryar fumbled the football deep in our own territory, and Denver recovered. The crowd went berserk! Soon, Denver scored a touchdown; they appeared reinvigorated. Our defense was discombobulated, and the need for oxygen increased. John Elway was relentless, and his team rallied around his leadership. We were in a heavy weight fight, and defeating the Broncos wouldn't be easy.

With only twelve minutes remaining in the contest, it was anybody's game. Each fan stood on their feet and screamed erratically; it was chaotic. Hearing the cadence from scrimmage was next to impossible. To adjust, we relied on auxiliary commands, but inadvertent infractions derailed our progress. Our game plan crumbled in the second half and Denver gained momentum. Tempers flared and untimely penalties buried us deeper into turmoil. Our frustration reached its climax when Denver scored and claimed the lead with minutes remaining in the game. We needed a touchdown, and I represented the team's final chance to score. I paced around the goal line waiting to receive the kickoff. My teammates applauded and directed their attention solely on me. The

fate of our season relied on special teams. It was a deep kick, and I back peddled to receive the ball near the end zone. Instantly, the lineman formed a wedge and I accelerated with the football up the field. Skillfully, I maneuvered around defenders and sprinted towards the end zone. The crowd stood paralyzed, while my teammates sprung up and down. I eluded two defenders before being shoved out of bounds near mid-field. It was just the break we needed. Our offense trotted onto the field with time running out. Unfortunately, a yellow flag was thrown on the field; it was a holding infraction. I was livid! Immediately, I challenged the referee's judgment; but it was to no avail. I ripped off my helmet and stared at the clock while the official marched us back towards our end zone. We needed a miracle. Grogan connected on first and second down, but it came to a crucial forth down play. We all held hands on the sideline and held our breath. Nevertheless, the Broncos prevailed and won a playoff berth as the final wild-card team. I felt so much pain. I cried while undressing in the locker room. That was the last time I undressed in a Patriots uniform.

The first person I called was dad. He told me that everyone in Jacksonville saw me on TV, and he never knew I cursed so much. We both laughed; it cheered me up after a disheartening defeat in Denver. I returned to Boston without a job, and my career was in limbo. Saying goodbye to Darryl was grievous, but we had arrived at different forks along our journey. However, we pledged to remain brothers forever. Renita and made preparations to leave town before the Christmas holiday. We had considered staying in Boston, but without a contract that thought quickly faded away.

The next morning, we crammed our valuables into our vehicles and headed south. The highways were congested with holiday travelers; driving was a nightmare. Suddenly, I noticed Renita lagging behind; she was barely moving. I knew that something was terribly wrong, and I feared the worst. I darted between commuters and found an exit ramp; luckily, there was a gas station on the corner. Minutes later Renita arrived with her hazard lights flashing. I plundered under the hood, but I had no idea what was wrong. Dusk was approaching and there was no one to help. Unannounced, an angel arrived and recommended a gas additive. I figured that it couldn't hurt, so I tried it. Within minutes we were on the road again.

Our next stop was at a rest area near Virginia. We were extremely tired and yearned a hot cup of coffee. Renita and I sat outside; we enjoyed being wooed by the pulsating sounds of night urchins. The next day we enjoyed a delectable Christmas dinner in Richmond; we even got a plate for Zeus.

It didn't take long to arrive in Jacksonville. The three of us stayed with mom in her apartment; we slept in one room, and mom and Stacy slept in the other. Zeus found a spot wherever he could. I enjoyed seeing my family and there was no place like home, but our plans to stay were temporary. Renita and I felt that it was the perfect time to start a family. We found a cute little apartment on the river; it was just minutes from mom. It didn't take long; soon I was informed that I was going to become a father. To celebrate we took a vacation.

We were both excited to visit Las Vegas; it was the honeymoon we never had. The Hacienda Hotel was immaculate; it was located on the far end of the strip. I had never gambled, but I was enticed to play the slot machines. Suddenly, I was startled by a loud noise. Bundles of coins tumbled from the machine; I had won the jackpot! Within seconds, security had arrived. Throngs of people watched as I collected my currency. It was an electrifying experience, and I wanted to win more. But hindsight altered my greed, and I decided to quit while ahead.

After a week in the wild wild west, it was time to return home; contract negotiations were rapidly approaching. Renita and I met with my new agent. Phil Williams and I analyzed my finance portfolio and discussed my career. Phil had identified a list of teams that inquired about my services. We concluded the meeting highly motivated. However, I devised a backup plan just in case football was no longer an option. Immediately, I enrolled into real estate school; my secondary plan was to become an investor. It was a drudging schedule, but the consequences were monumental.

The next day, I received a call from Bobby Grier. He confirmed that the organization was excited about my future, yet they elected not to protect me against free agencies. Those were bitter words to accept, and my ego was bruised. I was granted the opportunity to survey the market and sign with the highest bidder. That was the last time I talked with Coach Grier.

The first team to call me during the off-season was the Indianapolis Colts. I detested the notion of playing with the Colts; I wanted to play for a Super Bowl contender. The next inquiry came from the Minnesota Vikings. The Vikings were a formidable prospect, and I worked out for the team in Orlando. Unfortunately my efforts were curtailed by another pulled hamstring. My condition was abnormal. Never had I encountered such a problematic injury. I returned home with bad news. But more disturbing was the severity of my injury. Physically I was unable to perform. Days later Tom Donahue, the General Manager for the Pittsburgh Steelers, called to schedule a workout in Pittsburgh. I was thrilled. The Pittsburgh Steelers was a favorable choice, and they needed an elusive runner. I had two weeks to recover before auditioning in Pittsburgh.

Meanwhile, dad had to admit J into a convalescent home it was a tough decision, but her condition had degenerated; dad needed help. It was obvious by the expression on his face that he was deeply grieved. But to allow J to remain home would have been more grievous. J's new home was located on College St. She shared a tiny room with Mrs.

Williams on the second floor. Tragically, dad and I responded to an alarming phone call. The nursing home had transferred J to Riverside Hospital; her vital signs were failing. We panicked and rushed out of the house to render aid. The nurse informed us that J's blood pressure was barely registering; they didn't expect her to survive. We were advised by the doctor to make final arrangements. We were shocked! I walked outside to clear my mind.

Dad followed me and whispered, "My momma is going to be dead before sunset."

I was infused. I shouted, "Don't say that!"

The pain and fear had mounted. Timidly, we walked back into the hospital. Once inside, we gathered our composure and conferred our options with the medical staff. The doctor asked us for J's final wishes. We were uncertain.

We were burdened with the daunting task of asking my grandmother the most important question we had ever asked, "Do you want to be revived if your heart stops beating or would you rather die?"

The doctor also reminded us of her age and any pressure caused by resuscitation could crush J's fragile rib cage. Furthermore, there wasn't any guarantee that she would survive. I was under tremendous pressure, and it was vital that we make a decision fast; time was running out. I hugged daddy and took a deep breath. Gingerly, I walked toward J. Her heart monitor chirped at a sluggish pace. She was resting peacefully with her head slightly leaning to the side. I was afraid to wake her, but I had to. Gently, I rubbed her head and called out her name two or three times. Suddenly, she responded by blinking her eyes. Then, she barked out a cough and cleared her throat.

J looked into my eyes, they were filled with tears. I held her hand and sat beside her. She said, "Hey Joe."

Tears trickled down my cheek. Somehow, I summoned the courage to ask for her final wishes.

She responded in a raspy voice, "It's up to you, it doesn't matter."

I felt unqualified to adjudicate who lives or dies. Daddy and I decided to pray and ask God to intervene. It was a divine experience. God's spirit assured us of his presence. We were certain that our prayers had been answered. Miraculously, J's vital signs improved and she was dismissed from the hospital. However, the stress and pressure took its toll on dad. He commenced to drink and drive, and was apprehended by a police officer. His license was suspended. Dad had no choice but to ride his bicycle to see J. When his bike was stolen, he walked.

J's most glorious moments occurred while discussing her autographed team picture that was proudly displayed near her bedside. Frequently, I stopped by to visit; but on most occasions she was asleep. Patiently, I waited by her bedside until she awoke. Her face gleamed when she recognized that it was me. J maintained a hardy appetite, and I enjoyed feeding her dinner. I braced her sloping head with my hand and fed her blended food like an infant. Soon, she became lethargic and drifted asleep. J lay snuggled under her blanket. I turned on the radio to play her favorite gospel hymns. Then, I kissed her forehead. Before escaping from her room she mumbled, "So long Joe, so long!"

It shredded my heart into pieces.

J's caretaker was a compassionate worker with an effervescent spirit. Often, she'd serve beyond her call of duty to make life more enjoyable for the elderly. Thank you Miss Teresa, and may God bless you!

The following day, I flew into Pittsburgh. The winter solace brutally devoured the city; the land was barren. Abandoned steel factories stood paramount, reminding patrons of an era that was lost in time. However, the mighty Allegany River polarized the city. Its brown murky water crashed violently against the banks. Subsequently, I observed nomads walking nearby with duffle bags in their hands.

Once at Three Rivers Stadium, I met the legendary Chuck Knoll and mean Joe Green. As I walked past the trophy showcase I acknowledged the legacy of their winning tradition. Swiftly, I got dressed for workouts and met with the running back coach. Dick Hoak was a short middle aged man with an eye for talent; he was a man of few words. However, my hamstring restricted my mobility, and my performance faltered.

Nevertheless, the Steelers offered me a contract worth $130,000. I accepted their offer, but I planned on having a stellar season in order to negotiate for the big bucks the following season. The Pittsburgh Steelers were a great organization, and I was eager to start the season.

I returned to Jacksonville and prepared for training; minicamp was only a month away. I sold the Bronco and surprised Renita with a XJ6 Jaguar. Also, I donated 10% of my signing bonus to my church. To this day, they didn't know where the money came from; we remained anonymous.

Soon, I was back in Pittsburgh for minicamp. The team resided at a small college near the heart of the city. Duquesne was a haven for the intellectually astute. Also, it shared a winning basketball tradition that was nationally recognized. My roommate was a rookie defensive back from the University of Michigan. David Arnold and I got along extremely well. We drove through town listening to Easy E. Throngs of people polluted the streets wandering aimlessly. I asked David, "When do they go home?"

He replied, "This is their home."

David and I navigated through traffic and found our new home, Three Rivers Stadium. We shared the facility with the Pittsburgh Pirates. We comingled and became well acquainted with one another.

The teams most celebrated players were very humble. They made the adjustment for me pleasant; I loved my teammates.

After practices, we jogged in small groups into town. The fans were invigorated; they applauded and blew their horns. Offseason conditioning drills were exhausting, but I managed to survive. Frequently, the players patronized a campus pub and drank Iron City beer. I didn't like beer, but after a month in Pittsburgh I loved it; especially the way it made me feel. Other times, we partied at the O in Oakland. It was a popular spot at the University of Pittsburgh. Being a pro-athlete required lots of discipline. Every player was an open target for opportunists. David didn't stand a chance; he was lured to every pretty face that walked by. Lavished groupies congregated around the team hoping to attract the attention of a vulnerable rookie. On the weekends we paraded our luxury cars into Hyde Park and intermingled with the community.

Often, I'd drive into the hood for soul food. The hill district was a popular spot. It was a high crime drug infested area. Flaring cars allured the attention of undercover agents. On one occasion we were profiled as drug dealers, and angry serpents raided our vehicles with their weapons drawn. I sat perfectly still with my hands raised, while staring down the barrel of a gun. I was traumatized! Eventually, the cops recognized that they had made a mistake and we were free to go. That was the last time I ate soul food in Pittsburgh.

Brighter memories occurred when I drove home with David. Warren Ohio was a small town on the outskirts of Cleveland. It was nice getting away from camp, and I thoroughly enjoyed meeting David's family. They were very kind and hospitable. Later, at a family gathering, I met basketball legend Ron Harper; I was pleased to meet his acquaintance.

Also, I met one of the greatest defensive linemen in franchise history. We crossed paths in a popular night spot in Pittsburgh. He was a massive human being that towered above me. Nevertheless, he was aware of my reputation and wished me a successful season. I was honored to meet L.C. Greenwood.

Minicamp was coming to a conclusion, and the team decided to perform a stress test to evaluate the stability of my hamstring. I entered into our medical facility and was greeted by a tall gentleman standing near the treadmill detaching wires. He extended his hand and asked, "Are you Elgin?"

I extended my hand in return ad answered, "Yes I am."

Formally, he introduced himself and demanded me to strip into my underwear and tennis shoes. Then, I was subjected to a series of agonizing drills, starting with an intense sprint on the treadmill. I nearly passed out. My test results revealed that I suffered from high cholesterol. My physician customized a special diet and workout. It was prescribed to strengthen my hamstring and lower my cholesterol.

The next day, I packed my bags and flew into Jacksonville. I had a month before training camp, and I worked out feverishly. However, I was plagued by piercing pain; my hamstring relapsed. But, I gathered strength from an ailing woman. J epitomized greatness and an extraordinary will to survive. My daily visits to the convalescent home to visit her were greeted with adulation. Staff members fled their posts to sneak a peep at me. I was greatly flattered.

Quickly, training camp approached, and Renita and I prepared to return to Pittsburgh. Before leaving town, I was informed that Darryl had signed with our inter-conference rivals. The Cleveland Browns were an hour away from Pittsburgh, and we were scheduled to play against them in the preseason.

Renita was beginning to show the effects of her pregnancy. Driving made her feel nauseated and her lower extremities were beginning to swell. We made a pragmatic decision to put the cars on the auto train instead of driving. It was a wise choice; we both relaxed and viewed the countryside.

When we arrived in Pittsburgh the city had given birth to spring. Emerald foliage adorned the city, and it was clothed in a perfect wardrobe. The Steelers pointed us in the direction of Allegany Center. Upscale condos were located in the mall just miles away from Three River Stadium. Our condo, overlooking the city, was fully furnished with maid service. It was perfect for Renita; especially with the mall downstairs. Each day we ate shaved ice from the food court; peach and mango were my favorite. Sometimes, I bought two at a time, taking turns eating from each hand. It was a good thing that I didn't have more hands!

Pittsburgh was culturally enriching. Renita and I enjoyed an array of parks and museums, however, picnics were my favorite. Regardless of the adventure, my marriage was cultivating and it rewarded me with many everlasting memories.

The release of E.P.M.D.'s new album was greatly anticipated, and I was determined to buy the first copy and present it to Darryl as a token of our friendship. To remain in shape, I jogged up the stadium steps at Three Rivers; it was an arduous task. Tragically, I reinjured my hamstring and quad. Both muscles were severely swollen, and camp was only a week away. I was reluctant to report my injury to the medical staff in fear of their reaction. My strength coach was furious, and he demanded a full examination. John was very disappointed and he questioned my tactics. I referred to the old tactics back in New England. I poured Epson-salt in my hot tub and soaked for hours.

The next week I drove to Latrobe, PA for training camp. I prayed that my hamstring would endure four grueling weeks of camp. My roommate was physically intimidating. His lower torso was massive and he punished smaller defenders. Tracy Martin worked diligently to make a name for himself in the NFL, but he was plagued by injuries. Tracy and I made a perfect tandem. We enjoyed meaningful dialogue over dinner. However, Thursday nights were my favorite. I had a carnivorous appetite for seafood.

Morning practices were simple and brief. We avoided contact and concentrated on the mental aspect of the game. That catered to my advantage. I had plenty of time to rest and receive extra treatment. To the contrary, afternoon practice attracted hundreds of loyal fans. Chuck Knoll conducted a physical camp. We captivated the audience with bone shattering blows and blindside collisions. Most of the players limped into the training room for ice.

Training camp was going well; I had survived the first week. As I became more acclimated with the offense my confidence mounted. My performance commanded the attention of our coaching staff. Firmly, Dick gripped his clipboard and scanned the sideline. Unexpectedly, he yelled my name. I leaped to attention and grabbed my helmet. Seconds later, he screamed, "Get in there!"

My heart raced, and I joined my teammates in the huddle. Everyone was quiet except the quarterback; he was our leader. We broke the huddle with a handclap and I sprinted to my position. Standing directly in front of me was a ferocious linebacker. Soon, the quarterback called his cadence and the ball was snapped. I avoided contact and dashed up the field with a defender trailing. It was man coverage. Suddenly, I redirected my route, and the defender slipped and grabbed my jersey to regain his balance. The ball was thrown in my vicinity. Instinctively, I soared into the air and made a miraculous catch. The crowd stood and cheered, but I landed awkwardly. I felt a jolting pain in my leg and I labored walking off the field. Inconspicuously, I tried blending in among my teammates to conceal my identity; I was injured and didn't want to return. My aim was to reach the training room without anyone noticing. Nonetheless, Dick called my name minutes before practice ended. He demanded me to go in and run a special play. I couldn't refuse, my career was at stake. I made a solemn prayer and hoped to be used as a decoy. Instead, I received the football and sustained a brutal collision. I felt my hamstring rip further apart. Instantly, I clinched my leg and fell to the ground. I tried standing, but was unsuccessful. Soon, I was assisted off the field by a trainer. As a consequence, I missed the beginning of preseason.

I became paranoid after missing two consecutive games. I knew the business too well; three strikes and you're out! I couldn't afford to miss another game. Therefore, on my days off I remained on campus and received treatment; I had to get well. I had a slim chance of making the team, but time was ticking. I requested a Cortisone shot to ease the pain, but the Steelers were concerned that Cortisone could compound the problem. My appeal was denied.

I hobbled around camp with ice wrapped around my mangled hamstring. My faith was severely tried, and I blamed God for my misfortune. Soon, I noticed a significant improvement. The pain and swelling went away and I was able to walk without discomfort, but running was a greater challenge. Each day I became more persistent. I was determined to play in our next preseason game against the Cleveland Browns. I experienced restless nights. My mind was plagued with pessimistic thoughts; it was a living nightmare. After my teammates fell asleep, I ran sprints in the hall until I was able to tolerate the pain.

Days before the game, I met with Ralph for a final evaluation. He probe around my leg and asked, "How's it feel?"

I gave him a phony smile and replied, "Great!"

Ralph took my word and sanctioned me to practice. My running style was drastically altered to accommodate my hamstring. I made sure not to accelerate or make any abrupt turns. Nevertheless, I maintained a positive attitude and fought relentlessly to preserve my career.

The big game against Cleveland was a day away, and I was eager to see Darryl. He was delighted to hear that I was making the trip. We had a substantive conversation before concluding with a familiar salutation, "I love you yo!"

When we flew into Cleveland, our chartered bus awaited us on the runway. The team was escorted to our hotel; it stood majestically entrenched in the heart of town. I felt chills running down my spine; I was about to play the biggest game of my life against my dearest friend.

After breakfast, I scanned through my playbook and attended meetings. At 11:30, I ran to my room to call Darryl. He picked up the phone on the first ring. I was thrilled to hear his voice, he sounded great. I gave him the hotel address and my room number. Darryl said he was only minutes away, and that he'd see me around noon. I sat near the edge of my bed and waited impatiently. Soon, I changed the TV channel to Sports Center and previewed the weekend match-ups. That's when I glanced at the clock, it was 11:58. Then, I heard a soft knock on the door; it could only be one person. I suffered an adrenaline rush and bounced to my feet. I waltzed to the door with a smile on my face. Suddenly, I opened the door and there he stood, bigger than life, all 5'8" of him. He was well dressed and neatly groomed. Veins protruded from his biceps and calves; he looked unbelievable. I was exceedingly happy. We greeted each other with compassion and commenced to jabbing one another in the stomach. We wrestled on the bed like little kids. Our hearts had found home; nothing was bigger than our friendship.

The big game was several hours away, and I was eager to showcase Darryl to my teammates. We wandered into the lobby, and I noticed his Beamer. It was parked up front. I rushed outside to take a closer look; I gyrated around the car like a vulture over road kill. Darryl had installed custom rims; the car looked fabulous! Suddenly, Darryl threw me the keys. I sat inside and waited until the perfect moment to play E.P.M.D. Soon, Darryl became distracted by a fan and I eased it into the cassette player. Darryl paused. Then he shouted, "Oh no! It's E.P.M.D.!"

It was a special moment that was revered forever. It was just like old times. Darryl toured me around town, and then we stopped at Denny's for lunch. The restaurant was filled to capacity. Luckily, we found an empty seat nestled in the back of the restaurant. Darryl and I laughed and reminisced until our waitress arrived with menus. She had a warm and exuberant personality. Eventually, customers began to stare; Darryl's NFL paraphernalia disclosed his identity, and fans came over to greet us. However, there was so much that I needed to say to him before leaving. Minutes later, our waitress returned with our food; we both ordered burgers. Time was becoming a factor, and we had to eat fast. Our waitress was prompt; she presented our check and departed with a smile.

Finally, we were alone, and I felt a need to unleash my pain. I knew that Darryl could relate; he possessed the key to my heart. I sat with my arms crossed and confessed my fears; I expected him to console me. Instead, he wept and exhumed his demons. Darryl had been seduced by a beautiful temptress, and he compromised his fidelity. He was torn between two lovers and felt compelled to postpone his wedding plans with Mimi. Carla had infected his heart, and stimulated a deeper purpose to life. He described her as charming and articulate. I was unbiased as he pleaded his case and sought my endorsement. Then, a tear dropped from his eye. Darryl's passion for football had diminished, and his career was in great jeopardy. He was battling against the veteran receivers for one remaining spot on the team roster, and his chances of conquering appeared bleak.

On August 19, 1989, Darryl and I sat inside a clustered restaurant in Cleveland, Ohio and made a solemn oath…

We vowed to be our brother's keeper.

We vowed to become a beacon of light to those that were in darkness.

We vowed to become servants of God.

We vowed to feed the hungry, shelter the homeless, and clothe the naked.

We vowed to become loyal husbands to our wives, and honor our wedding vows.

We vowed to become the God-fathers of each other's children.

We vowed to become neighbors, and grow old with dignity and honor.

We vowed to become business men, and serve our community.

We vowed to retire at the end of the season, and walk away with dignity.

We vowed to raise our children upright, and build a legacy that our offspring would inherit.

Then, we dried our eyes and walked out in unity.

My experience at Cleveland Stadium was exhilarating. The moment that I stepped into the locker room I felt a glorifying mystique. Chuck Knoll was a master motivator. He delivered an energetic speech that brought chills to my spine. However, my duties were relegated to special teams. Tightly, I wrapped my hamstring and found a vacant stall in the bathroom to pray for me and Darryl. Then, I trotted onto the field and joined my teammates. The fans were rambunctious. Some masqueraded near the end zone wearing dog masks, others waved bones; that section of the stadium was known as the dog pound.

Darryl looked great returning punts; he made a strong campaign to make the team. The contest was extremely intense, and I was relieved that Darryl and I didn't have to battle against each other; that would've broken my heart. In spite of the game's outcome, I considered myself victorious. I survived without reinjuring my hamstring.

After returning to Pittsburgh, the team broke camp. I rejoiced and joined Renita at our apartment at Allegany Center. Our next opponent was the Philadelphia Eagles. As the regular season approached, the support players were gradually phased out. In contrast, the starters were implemented into practice more regularly. It was disheartening to see that my name had been removed from among the special teams. That indicated that my time as a Steeler was nearly over. Each day I observed practice from the sideline with a wounded ego. I conceded to defeat, and I wondered how to explain my failure to Renita and the rest of my family. I prepared Renita for the worst; she was aware that I could get released at any time. I thank God for Renita. She made me feel special in spite of a gloomy forecast.

Later that week, I flew in with the team to Philadelphia. I had an eerie feeling in my spirit; I knew that my hamstring had sealed my fate. My emotions ranged from grief to guilt. I thought about the Cortisone shots I received, and wondered if it was a prudent idea. However, I was happy that the rookies were getting an opportunity to play. Especially Eric Wilkerson; he was a promising runner from Kent State.

The players boarded the team bus burdened with tension; no one uttered a word. Most of the guys were uncertain about their odds of making the team. However, a good performance would more than likely secure a future in the NFL. I occupied my time meditating and reflecting on my journey. Soon, the bus came to a stop, and I beheld Veteran Stadium.

The mystique of ancient rivalries marked its authenticity. The locker room was memorialized by the sweat and blood of would be opponents. However, Chuck Knoll reminded us of our mission. We pledged to return victorious. I wore my Steelers uniform with pride, and I petitioned God to protect me and Darryl. Then, I trotted onto the field with my teammates. We were greeted by an angry crowd, but our confidence prevailed. I paced the sidelines recklessly awaiting my chance to play. Bodies and helmets flew around like bullets as the play clock ticked.

Half time had come and gone, and I still hadn't touched the field; my career was drifting away. Angrily, I watched one running back after another enter into the game. I was livid! I felt defeated when Eric Wilkerson entered the game in the fourth quarter and scored a touchdown. He was mobbed in the end zone by zealous teammates.

My chances of making the squad were severely crippled; I needed to match his performance. But time was my enemy; there were only minutes left to play.

I relied on our defense to come up with a big play; it was my only chance of playing. Suddenly, the defense recovered a fumble, and the offense trotted onto the field with under two minutes to play. I leaped up with my helmet and ran next to Dick Hoak. I felt my heart drop as my dreams faded away with each tick of the clock. Then, I was urged to go into the game with seconds to play. I hoped to receive the football on the final play of the game but, my dreams ended in disappointment. Rather, I watched our quarterback kneel down and end the game. However, I held my head high and walked away from Veteran Stadium representing the Steelers and my family with dignity and pride.

Section IV: Midnight

Immediately, the team returned to Pittsburgh and prepared for practice. Unfortunately, it was a grievous moment. Some of my teammates had come to the end of their careers. I sat in the locker room and watched my friends receive the traumatic news. My heart sweltered and I wondered who was next. Soon, my curiosity was fulfilled; the next person was me.

The news pierced my soul and rendered me speechless. I sat motionless with my head slumped between my knees. I fought away the tears and tried to regain my composure. Suddenly, my teammates gathered around and strengthened me with their love. It was difficult saying goodbye to the game that I dedicated my entire life to. But, somehow I found the fortitude to pick up my pride and walk towards the door. The last person I greeted was Eric Wilkerson; he was dressing for practice.

Tom Donahue's office was down the hall. Discretely, I entered into his office with my playbook in hand. Surprisingly, he was deeply disturbed by my pain, and he regretted telling me that my hamstring had derailed my progress. I accepted my misfortune and thanked him for the opportunity.

I left Three Rivers Stadium in my Jag listening to E.P.M.D. I prayed that Darryl had received promising news. When I arrived home, Renita was ecstatic; she had found a new job downstairs. But I stood aloof staring out of the window. Never had I experienced the sorrow of rejection. Intuitively, she knew that something was terribly wrong. She grabbed my hand and looked at me with her beautiful brown eyes. I didn't have to say much; she had prepared for the worse. I felt awful, but Renita's attitude was resilient. During this turbulent moment, she remained optimistic. Her faith in God was unperturbed.

The next day, Auntie called; she had read about my misfortune in the local newspaper. However, my family's support was monumental. Mom and dad helped me to regain hope. Shortly, we left Pittsburgh and headed towards Jacksonville.

Casually, we drove through the Allegany Mountains and headed south. Soon, we were dazzled by bright lights and skyscrapers. New York City was engulfing! Hostile motorists blared their horns while street peddlers begged for coins. While cruising through the Bronx, our luxury vehicle attracted the stares of strangers. Our safety became a major concern. Quickly, I raised my window and locked the doors. However, navigating through traffic and finding I-95 was a dilemma. I stopped for directions, but was led deeper into chaos; something was awry. Luckily, I found a cop and was assisted out of danger.

We returned to Jacksonville and moved in with my in-laws. Their guest bedroom became our new home. I had anticipated getting resigned with another team, but I was greatly mistaken. The ramification drastically detoured the course of my life. Everybody did their best to elevate my spirit. The dissention of my career effected daddy severely. Sometimes, I caught him staring into space with a troubled look on his face. Other times, he gulped Gin straight out of the bottle, followed by Coca-Cola. I was disheartened and felt I had compromised my family's future. I had placed the burden of alleviating decades of destitution on my shoulders, but I failed miserably. Feverishly, I searched for a family business to buy. I needed big money to meet my financial obligations.

I met with business brokers on a daily basis. Many propositions were tempting, but their offers came at an inopportune time. Renita was beginning to have complications with her pregnancy, and my presence was needed. We attended doctor visits and natural birth classes; it was a cultivating experience. However, football demonized me; I was tortured night and day. Skeptics inundated me with a barrage of questions that

I couldn't answer. I hated football. Privately, I sat and watched my peers fulfill their ambitions and entertain the world. I critiqued and evaluated each players performance, especially the running backs.

Often, I yelled, "You've got the ball in the wrong hand!"

My heart became bitter, and I envied my peers. I felt cheated out of a career, and cringed at the sight of their follies.

Each day I waited by the phone hoping that it would ring; I longed for a second chance. But no team expressed interest in my services. The NFL season was well into October and a plethora of teams were decimated by injuries. The Miami Dolphins were my best prospect. They were desperate for a runner and I was a prime candidate. Quickly, I seized the opportunity and called the team's general manager. Minutes later, the Dolphins arranged my flight schedule.

I was thrilled. The news resurrected joy within my family. While getting dressed the phone rang. Quickly, I ran to answer; it was the Miami Dolphins. The news was heart breaking; they had reneged on their offer. Apparently, my health problems were systematic, and the Dolphins wanted no part. I was embarrassed to tell my family; I was humiliated, but they noticed a change in my countenance. Unfortunately, grief and sorrow became familiar companions throughout the year, often appearing with little or no sign at all. That day was no exception my family mourned with me, and I accepted the grim reality that football was no longer an option.

Shortly after, Renita and I searched for a house of our own. We found the perfect little condo; it was nestled near the banks of the St. Johns River. Mom was delighted to have me at home, but hated seeing me in agony; it was too much for her to bear. Slowly, I drifted into isolation and drank liquor to ease the pain. Loved ones tried to mend my broken heart, but the wound was too deep. It was dehumanizing being mocked and castigated by members of society.

Immediately, I began looking for a job. I figured that my influence would be greatly accepted among the job market. But every reputable company denied my application; they required a college degree. I battled against my ego and accepted a modest job to absorb our financial deficit. I felt worthless. Getting acclimated to life without football was devastating. Anger persuaded my judgment and I perceived society as my adversary. It was difficult to ascertain why a popular personality was rejected.

Meanwhile, Darryl's future loomed bright. After being released by the Browns, the San Diego Chargers signed him. Our plans as businessmen were temporarily postponed. But nearly as fast as he had arrived, Darryl was gone; he only lasted a couple of weeks. Finally, it looked as if Darryl was on his way to Florida, but the Arizona

Cardinals derailed his route and signed him to a contract. Darryl raved about playing for the Cardinals, and he assured me that his success was inevitable. I was overjoyed to hear the renewed passion in his voice, and I became his biggest fan.

On Sundays, Renita and I glued our eyes to the TV. We treasured watching Darryl play; he was a feisty competitor. Darryl and I conversed several times a week, and I ranted and raved over his performance. Occasionally, I made a caricature of his big lips; he laughed hysterically.

Darryl tried to entice me to work out for the Cardinals; he was adamant about my chances of making the team. However, I wanted no part of the NFL. Darryl reconfirmed his pledge and insisted that I look for more business opportunities. Darryl remained in Arizona at the conclusion of the season for offseason workouts, and the bulk

of our plans were relegated to me. It was a tedious process, but I found the perfect business. Darryl embraced the idea of owning a Domino's Pizza franchise. It was in a prime location and it yielded a great profit. But the condo next door was more tantalizing. It was on the market, and moderately priced to provoke a quick sale. I had to act swiftly on Darryl's behalf, because the property was beginning to attract prospects.

Meanwhile, Renita had entered into the final stages of her pregnancy, and the effects had reached its zenith. Renita's belly had protruded enormously and her mobility was severely restricted. In spite of her physical changes, she was absolutely beautiful, and catering to her needs cultivated my manhood. To help induce labor, we'd walk around the neighborhood for exercise. On other occasions, I'd rub her tummy with cocoa-butter to soothe tension; she loved that. However, the most consecrated moments occurred at night during prayer. Gently, I'd cradle Renita's stomach and make supplications. Amazingly, the baby would respond by kicking; it was miraculous! Instantly, I felt a deeper connection and rededicated my life to serve my family.

The following day I invited my loved ones to dinner at Red Lobster. It was the first time we ate out as a family since I signed my scholarship back at UCF. We gathered around the largest table and reminisced over our favorite entrees. It was a night to revere. Suddenly, Renita looked uncomfortable. She complained about experiencing gas pains.

Everyone was concerned. Immediately, we prepared to leave. The family escorted us out until we were safely in the vehicle.

While heading home, the pains increased and Renita's discomfort became more obvious. I tried to maintain my cool, but the thought of Renita giving birth was alarming. Cautiously, I drove through every red light; then accelerated to top speeds with my hazard lights blinking. Luckily, we arrived home unscathed. I quickly gathered Renita's bags and called mom; I was in a rampage. Renita gripped her stomach and endured thrashing pain.

Shortly after midnight, Renita was admitted into Humana Hospital in Orange Park. Her labor pains were twenty minutes apart, and she began to dilate. Calmly, I sat adjacent to her bed and caressed her hand; sharp pains tortured her. Minutes later, Mr. and Mrs. Reed arrived. It was a restless night; sleep eluded us all. As morning approached, Renita's pain occurred more frequently. She squandered from side to side and demanded an epidural to alleviate the pain. Her facial expressions were the bitter images of agony. Quickly, I ran to get the nurse.

We were informed about the birth procedure and given green gowns with little hats to put on; the time was nigh. Then, the assaulting pain ushered the baby's arrival. Renita cried in travail. Mr. Reed rushed to her bedside and doused her head with a cool cloth.

The nurse yelled, "Push, push!"

Mrs. Reed whispered, "Nita, you're doing great!"

Renita was fatigued, and panted for air. Quickly, I feed her ice chips to moisten her parched mouth. Suddenly, the pain reemerged. She gripped the bedrails and pushed until she gave birth. Immediately, the doctor gave me the scissors to cut the umbilical cord.

On February 25, 1990 around 9:36AM, Renita gave birth to Angelica La'che Davis, a 6 lb 7 oz little girl. I stood in awe as I reached for my baby girl that was covered in child birth. It was impossible to fathom being a father; but it was glorifying! Mr. Reed was extremely honored; it was his birthday.

Tightly wrapped in a pink blanket, I waltzed Angelica around the room. It was the greatest day of my life. Suddenly, the phone rang, and I rushed to answer. Surprisingly it was Auntie. Seconds later, I dropped the phone and stood paralyzed. I was lambasted with horrifying news. I heard Auntie call out, "Elgin are you there?"

Slowly, I backed away and mumbled, "No. No."

Eventually, I stumbled into the wall making ruckus. Renita was startled. She gazed at me with wrinkles creased in her forehead.

Frantically, she screamed, "What's wrong? What's wrong?"

I paused while tears rolled down my eyes. Then, I approached her and said, "Darryl's dead. My best friend is dead."

Renita was shocked! She closed her eyes and thrashed her head back against the pillow screaming, "No! No!"

Tears poured from her eyes. I had a new life in one hand, while receiving death on the other. It was the most painful and bitter moment of my life. Finally, tears fell from Angelica's eyes, and we cried together. I gave the baby to the nurse and got home as fast as I could to call Darryl's house, but no one answered. I tried calling again and again. Finally I reached Mrs. Usher. When she answered I knew that something terrible had happened; she was hysterical. Mrs. Usher lamented uncontrollably and uttered these words, "Darryl is dead. My son is dead."

Her pain was inconceivable.

Both Darryl and his girlfriend were brutally murdered by a deranged lunatic, whose mind disintegrated into a state of psychosis. Craig Gardner, a jealous thug, entered into Darryl's apartment and unloaded six bullets into his body. Then, he reloaded and shot his ex-girlfriend to death before taking his own life.

It was one of the most horrific murders in NFL history. Darryl C. Usher was pronounced dead on February 24, 1990, in Phoenix,

Arizona. He was only twenty five and left behind his mother, Ulma Usher, brothers, Raymond, Michael, Paul, and a host of family members and friends. Darryl was laid to rest in San Mateo, California in Sky Line Cemetery. Here is an account of the actual 911 report:

On a Saturday morning at 11:26, City of Phoenix emergency operator Belinda Banda received a 911 call from Chiquita Burt, who said, "Someone just keeps harassing me...he's threatening to do something to my boyfriend's car." The "someone," she explained, was Craig Gardner, who was unhappy that she had broken off their relationship.

Burt told the operator that Gardner had tried to assault her at a nightclub the previous evening. He threatened to kill her and her family. She went to the Tempe and Phoenix police to get a restraining order, but was told that she would have to wait until the courts opened the following Monday. During the night, Gardner had tried to locate her, twice showing up at a friend's residence in the morning hours. Burt fled to the apartment of her new boyfriend, Darryl Usher, a professional football player.

She told Banda that Gardner knew where Usher lived and had called saying that he was coming over to "do something" to Usher's car. The 911 operator asked if Gardner was an ex-boyfriend. "Yeah, he is," she answered. "And um, my boyfriend (Usher) said if he comes over here, he's gonna shoot him."

Burt asked what she could do to deal with Gardner. Banda briefly described the process for obtaining a restraining order.

Burt responded: "But I'm talking about, about right now. What can I do?"

Banda: "Where does he live? Nearby or something?"

Burt: "Yeah, he lives close."

Banda: "Well, how close is close to where you're at now?"

Burt: "I'm like five minutes, not even five minutes away."

The 911 operator obtained the address Burt was calling from, including the apartment complex name and building number. Twice in the ensuing minutes, Banda told Burt that she would be sending an officer.

"Well, we can have an officer come out there and take some information. If he happens to show up, though, before an officer gets there, you need to call us right away, okay, and tell us he's there now."

Burt repeated her concern that trouble might be brewing because of Gardner's threats and pursuing her all night. "And I'm—I'm just trying to prevent somebody from getting hurt."

Banda concluded the call by saying: "Okay, well, we'll send an officer out there, um like I said, if he happens to show up at the apartment before the officers first do, just call us back right away, okay?"

Twenty-two minutes after Burt's call to 911, Craig Gardner went through the front window of Usher's apartment and fatally shot both Darryl Usher and Chiquita Burt.

Then he put the gun to his head and killed himself.

The victims' mothers brought wrongful death actions against the City of Phoenix for handling of the 911 call. The plaintiffs claimed that the city was liable because the operator had improperly categorized Burt's call as Priority 3, the Phoenix Police Department's lowest rating, reserved for "service" or "report" calls of crimes after the fact. During the period, Priority 3 calls had an average response time of 32.6 minutes. Priority 1, or emergency "hot" calls for crimes in progress posing a threat of immediate personal danger, had an average response time of 4.4 minutes. Priority 2 calls, often used for domestic violence incidents, averaged 13.6 minutes.

The plaintiffs also alleged that Banda had negligently failed to prepare and convey a supplemental dispatch card to police radio personnel according to departmental policy, further hampering a response. When witnesses at Usher's apartment called 911 to report the shooting, Phoenix police arrived on the scene within seven minutes.

The jury found the city negligent and awarded Burt's mother $600,000, and Usher's mother $1.1 million. The jury assigned seventy-five percent of the liability to the city. The defense moved alternatively for a new trial, a remittitur, or judgment notwithstanding the verdict. The trial judge denied all motions and the city appealed.

The court of appeals affirmed the liability and damage verdicts, but reversed and remanded for a new trial on the appointment of fault, concluding: "The evidence does not justify a verdict that the 911 operator was three times as much at fault for the wrongful deaths of plaintiffs' decedents as Gardner, who intentionally shot and killed the plaintiffs' decedents."

Elgin Davis

Often, I wondered what Darryl's final thoughts were, as each bullet pierced into his body. I can't begin to say how much his death affected me. But, it's suffice to say that meeting him enriched my life, and a part of his spirit is enlarged deeply within my heart. The world was robbed of an incredible human. He had had a love for life and God, and he transformed those around him. Darryl was an angel among us. Often I wonder what he would've named his children. He might have had a son to follow in his footsteps, or a beautiful little girl like Angelica. Darryl never fulfilled his vow to become a godfather to my girls, became my next door neighbor, or my business partner. However, he left behind a much greater gift; Darryl Usher left me with hope.

Darryl's death was difficult to accept, and I lived in denial. I continued calling him every Tuesday as I had done for months before the shooting. I listened to his voice on his answering machine, hoping this was all just a dream and that he'd answer the telephone. I called until his phone was disconnected. I never gave up hope for a miracle.

Darryl's mom suffered miserably; often she'd speak in a defeated tone, short of breath. She was loved and supported by the Cardinals organization and many other grievous players throughout the NFL. The nation was traumatized by the tragedy. Shortly after Darryl's death, Mrs. Usher traveled to Alaska and various parts of the far-east to cope with her loss. Before leaving she wanted me to have Darryl's car, which he loved so much. Nevertheless, I decided that it should stay with her.

I had nightmares and many restless nights. One night I was awaken by a terrifying dream. Somewhat dazed and confused, I fixated on a particular object sitting in my living room; it resembled a person, Craig Gardener. I leaped out of bed enraged, and bolted towards the object screaming violently; I wanted to avoid another tragedy. Halfway there, I felt a rip in my hamstring, but I continued with a vengeance. As I approached, I noticed that it was just a lamp. I turned around and limped back to bed with another pulled hamstring.

We all suffered in our own way, but never had I experienced anything as strange as the night of May 9, 1990. Between the hours of 3AM and dawn, I was in a trance-like state. The presence of a light beam formed a vertical tunnel directly over me. It had a vacuum like effect. It was drawing life right out of my body. I felt unbearable pressure centered around my head. It felt like my brain was being sucked right out. I fought with all my strength and tried calling for help, but I couldn't utter a sound. I was paralyzed, fighting an internal battle that went on for about two or three minutes. Sometimes I felt like giving up because I was mentally exhausted. But I was afraid of where my spirit would go and if I would return into my body, and I fought to stay. Then, the light was gone. I woke up hyperventilating and drenched in sweat. I called out to Renita for aid. She doused my forehead with a damp cloth until I regained my composure. I remained conscious and drank cold water until sun rise. The next night it returned again around the same time, I experienced all of the effects of the previous night. I was left with so many unanswered questions about what had happened. I have never experienced another episode since then, and I can't explain it. My experience was real and not a dream. I'm sure if my spirit was taken that night I would have experienced something uniquely divine, and it would've defied logic. I've come to a hypothesis about what happened that night. However, I choose not to disclose that belief. It will remain between me and God.

Angelica's birth balanced our pain, and she filled our house with love and joy. Our family and friends made frequent stops to visit the baby. My greatest joy, however, came when I took Angelica to the convalescent home to see J for the very first time. It was like watching the east and west emerge as one. The sun set on J now nearly 91, but rose again with Angelica. I watched J hold Angelica with a mother's tender touch, while staring into her eyes. What a historic sight, the young and weak, and the old and fragile both represent beauty in their opposite spectrums of life. Before I grabbed Angelica from J's fatigued arms, I felt the bond being transmitted one to the other.

The entire family took turns helping us with the baby, especially mom and Mrs. Reed. Sometimes they spent the night so that Renita could rest; it couldn't have come at a better time. Unexpectedly, the Winnipeg Blue Bombers, of the Canadian Football League, signed me to a two year contract. I left my family behind and headed up north to salvage what little career I had left, and dedicated the season to Darryl. Canada was beautiful, but bitterly cold. The rules of the game were a little different and the size of the field was a lot bigger. I seldom socialized. It was strictly business. I dressed everyday for practice by writing Darryl's name on a piece of tape across the front of my shoulder pads; I positioned it right over my heart. During the first week my teammates called me Darryl. They must have thought I was the meanest guy on the team because I never responded; I wasn't use to people calling me Darryl. I had an impressive camp. However, without any explanation, Mike Riley cut me from the team. I was baffled, angry, and offended. Two days later, I arrived in Jacksonville and knocked on my front door. Again, Renita bandaged my wounds.

That was the first of many doors slammed shut. We lived off of our savings for nine months, and our finances were evaporating quickly. I settled for odd jobs here and there, while trying to hold onto my pride. Many people gossiped and whispered unkind words that crippled and handicapped my spirit. I isolated myself and slipped into depression, feeling sorry for myself and wondering how this could have happened to me. Where did I go wrong? I thought that my God, my friend, and my savior had abandoned me. Often, I gathered up loose change from around the house to purchase a 40oz of Old Milwaukee Best. I walked a mile to the little store while Renita and the baby slept. Most nights I sat on the curb side in front of the house getting a buzz. I reflected on the life that I had lost. It was too much to bear. I was decaying internally, and suicide thoughts plagued my mind. I smiled in front of friends and family, trying to uphold my dignity and pride. But I cried on the inside, and thought that my life was over. Frequently, I asked God, "Will I ever be resurrected, and return to glory?" I had serious doubts, and my confidence was shattered.

The most painful part was disappointing the people I had loved most. I watched dad fall into alcoholism once again. Anything could trigger the urge and losing my career didn't make things any better. He was a grieving father who constantly worried about me. He wanted me to have the things in life that he never had. I tried to be strong for him, while silently I suffered. Mom and dad were depending on me. Instead of me coming to their rescue, they came to mine with money to help with the bills and pocket change for the baby. It was dehumanizing; my manhood was shattered. But daddy and mom always knew the right words to say. They kept my spirit and heart focused on God.

Late one night while watching TV, I heard Ted Koppel introduce his next guest on Night Line. Minister Louis Farrakhan was described as the controversial leader of the Nation of Islam. I thought that it was a strange name, especially for a black man. But his message completely transformed my life. I heard the voice of God speaking through him. His message soothed my pain and hurt that was caused by years of injustice and misfortune. The Minister charismatically spoke words of wisdom without fear. I was mesmerized by his appearance and his soft spoken manner. He manifested a foreign power that represented salvation. I felt a spiritual kinship calling me out of darkness and into the light. The next day while listening to the radio, I heard a lecture by Minister Farrakhan. It was the most powerful message that I had ever heard. Immediately, I ordered the tape and it was personally delivered to me by one of the Muslim sisters. She was ornately dressed in an unorthodox garment. Silk fabrics draped across her shoulders. Sister O'Sheen had an aura that projected wisdom. She offered me a book and additional information about Minister Farrakhan; I was intrigued.

I was eager to inform my family and friends about my experience, but it was quickly dismissed as bane rhetoric, especially among the Christian community. I was taken back, and couldn't understand how a message that gave me hope and inspiration could be embraced with so much bitterness. I wasn't looking for a new religion, only the truth that would set me free.

The following Sunday, Renita and I were invited to the Mosque; it was located in an urban community center. I parked in the back row and observed a disciplined group of men neatly dressed in dark suits and bow ties. They resembled soldiers in the military. I was captivated, but extremely reluctant to attend service; it was much different than I was accustomed to attending.

Renita said, "Are you getting out?"

I said, "No." Then we drove out of the parking lot.

The next day, I received a call from my agent, Phil Williams. He informed me about a new international football league. The World Football League served as a farm league for the NFL, and it showcased a plethora of talent. The best news was that they had an interest in me, in spite of my lingering injuries. With a dwindling job market and an exhausted bank account, I was forced to return to football. I had a week to prepare for workouts, and I decided to revisit the Mosque before leaving.

I wore my finest suit and walked boldly toward the Mosque entrance. The brothers greeted me with the salutation of peace, As Salaam Alaikum. I didn't understand Arabic, but fortunately one of the brothers was a football fan and recognized me. Brother Eric told me what it meant. The brothers embraced me openly and made me feel at home. The brothers were superbly groomed, and their faces resembled the light of day. I was highly impressed by the kind and gentle words that exuded from their mouths. But more than anything, they were perfect ambassadors of the community. Once inside I surrendered to a search procedure. Any object that was harmful to self and others was confiscated until the meeting was over. Even cigarettes were prohibited in the Mosque. Then, the men were seated separate from the women. I found that strange, especially when I didn't notice a choir or organ. I felt like it was my first day of school all over again. But what came out of Minister Earl's mouth aroused my curiosity for knowledge like never before. I learned about the history of the original black man and the facts of creation. Minister Earl lectured about the earth 66 trillion years ago and how the moon was once part of the earth. He taught me that the hog was a forbidden meat to eat since it was grafted rat, cat and dog. And that God had come to save the poor and rejected black men and women of North America. I didn't completely understand it all, nor did I understand Islam. But I had heard enough to want to investigate. I greeted the brothers and left with a bean pie and several books.

When I arrived to Orlando, the Citrus Bowl was filled with gladiators and legendary coaches. My heart began to race, and I was eager to redeem my career. I was well known and respected among the players. I even had a chance to meet Tom Landry. The weather was perfect, and I felt great. Having NFL experience served to my advantage, and I was expected to be a top pick in the draft. The drills were organized and conducted perfectly. I was assigned to a small group near midfield. Thoroughly, I stretched my hamstring and prepared to run the forty yard dash. Suddenly, my name was called. I hopped to my feet and approached the starting line in trepidation. I took a deep breath and got into a comfortable sprinter stance. A dozen or more coaches gathered around the finish line with their stop watches. Suddenly, someone yelled, "Come on Elgin!"

My heart was pounding. Then, I exploded out of my stance and accelerated towards the finish line in perfect form. Just before finishing the race, I heard a pop. Immediately, I lost my balance and fell towards the ground gripping my hamstring. My day was done, and the draft was less than 24 hours away. I had blown my last opportunity and now I was at the mercy of whatever team would take a chance on me.

Around 4PM, the World Football League conducted its first draft in a hotel ballroom downtown. Hundreds of players nervously awaited their fate. I sat among an esteemed group of athletes, and watched most of them get selected. Three rounds had past, and no one chose me. History was repeating itself; I didn't know how much more I could take. When I thought that hope was lost, my name was called. I was selected by the London Monarchs in the fourth round. The crowd erupted when my picture appeared on the TV monitor.

The news brought cheers among my family, but when I told them it was London, I got silent. I reminded everyone, especially Renita, that it was temporary and it could lead back to the NFL. The training camp lasted for two weeks, but my injury restricted me to a lack luster performance. I was a step slower and less agile. I had become acclimated to playing with pain. My family was the only thing that kept me fighting; we needed the $2,000 weekly salary. I finished camp without sustaining any additional injuries. It was a valiant effort, but once again I was cut.

I left Orlando with a mountain of debt. Bill collectors called and threatened to take the cars and the house. The stress was unbearable. Often, I'd toss and turn at night. I didn't know where to turn for help. My greatest joy occurred while listening to Minister Farrakhan. To my surprise, the Mosque had appointed a new minister. Eddie was a meek man, standing only 5'7". His thick bifocal lenses sat clumsily on his face. He had a passion and love for helping Minister Farrakhan awaken the oppressed masses. His love for knowledge was nurtured at Harvard law School. He was articulate, and his exegesis of scripture was captivating, controversial, and revolutionary.

I absorbed more knowledge in the Mosque than any other place of higher learning. Islam made me feel whole and gave me a purpose to live. Furthermore, I was able to ascertain complex truths to help cope with the vicissitudes that were affecting my life. I was drowning in a sea of ignorance and deception. That day, a life preserver was offered and I accepted Islam as my religion. I felt born again. It gave me faith, hope, and love within myself; I saw life through a different prism. Football and all of its problems appeared trivial compared to God's love and purpose. I purchased my first Holy Quran and learned the Muslim prayer, bearing witness that there is no God but Allah and that Muhammad is his messenger. The more knowledge I received the more I wanted to share with others. I started attending meetings throughout the week on a regular basis. Also, I gave up pork, alcohol, and ate one meal a day. My friends and family noticed a change in my behavior. My language changed from cursing and swearing to a reformed tongue of cleanliness. My mind was relieved of its burden, as I gave all my hurts and problems of the past to Allah (God). Never had I experienced such peace. I appealed to Renita that she join the Mosque, but to my surprise Islam was grotesquely rejected. Contention and strife grew within my home, and I began my spiritual journey alone.

Days later, Phil Williams called with good news. He informed me that the World League wanted me back as an alternate player. I had to attend the practice and rehabilitation facility in Dallas, TX and compete with other athletes for an opportunity to earn a spot with a permanent team. There was a significant difference in pay. Team Dallas players earned a measly $500 per week. However, the salary increased to $2,000 per week when placed on a team. I accepted the offer; we needed the money.

Once in Dallas, quickly I emerged as one of the highlights of the team. Coaches and players wondered why someone with my ability wasn't playing in the NFL. Each player was observed and evaluated on film, which was sent to each team in the World League. Every Monday, new players were selected and flown out to teams throughout the league. Those that weren't selected kept on practicing hard and hoped for better news the following Monday. Most times, I stayed inside my hotel room reading the Quran or listening to the Minister. Sometimes, I'd walk with friends to the Irvin Mall; it was minutes from my room. I looked forward to pay day. My family was struggling and they were depending on me. Each night I called home and told Renita and the baby that I loved them.

After taxes, I brought home $461, but I lived off of $61 a week. I sent $400 home to Renita. I couldn't wait for Mondays, as I expected to be the next player to leave. But one player after another was chosen before me. I patiently watched others dreams become a reality while my dreams faded away. The best part of the experience was getting dressed in the locker room before and after practice. Each player rejoiced in a familiar environment, in their own way. I enjoyed listening to the boom box and watching the guys dance and clown around. I never rejected a good laugh or friendly competition on the field. Nevertheless, my body was taking a pounding. Sometimes I could barely walk; my joints were severely inflamed. I contemplated quitting, but I was broke and my family needed every penny.

To relieve my pain I filled the bathtub with ice and water. It was unbearable, but I found the strength to soak my entire body until it was numb. That became my nightly ritual for eight grueling weeks. Unfortunately, I never received a call from one team, but I held onto hope as long as I could. Eventually, I was forced to concede that my dream wouldn't come true as the season came in an abrupt end.

There were many uncomfortable and frightening thoughts that invaded my mind while flying back to Jacksonville, but I was blessed to have a beautiful family to embrace. Renita nursed and nourished my wounded ego back once again. Angelica had blossomed, she was up and walking. Mom was doing great with a new job and looking to buy her first house, while J and daddy both struggled with life in their own unique ways.

My most rewarding moment occurred with my grandmother. I decided to surprise her with a fish fry; it was J's favorite southern treat. Renita called the fish market and ordered two dozen fresh water Brim. She made sure that they were cleaned with the heads left on. That's the way J liked them. I had informed the convalescent home that I would be arriving to pick up J. When I pulled into the parking lot, she was gracefully sitting in her wheelchair wearing a white dress with a shawl draped across her shoulders. I approached her with a smile on my face, like a groom in pursuit of his bride. It was a touching moment. Some nurses even cried while I wheeled her out to the Jaguar. While lifting J into the front seat, I made sure to be extremely careful; but the pain was unbearable. She screamed, "Stop! Stop!"

The staff attempted to offer assistance, but I strategically maneuvered J's crippled and swollen legs into the car. As we drove, J looked astounded. The city's main thoroughfare revealed breathtaking views of rose pastures, and rivers flowed nearby. No one said a word as I drove, avoiding bumps and pot holes along the way.

Then she looked at me and said, "Joe, you got it made!"

Tears rolled down my face when I thought of how great God was to bless us with this moment in time. J was 92 years old, born a sharecropper. She hustled and worked odd jobs here and there to make ends meet during a time when discrimination and racism inherited the land, and justice stood far away. Twenty-six years later her only grandson achieved the unthinkable and fulfilled the prayers of her dreams.

Slowly, I wiped away my tears and said, "No J, we got it made. It's because of you, and the things you taught me that made me the man I am today. Thank you J!"

She replied, "You're welcome Joe!"

I was honored to be her grandson. Once we arrived home, she received a hero's welcome. Renita greeted J with the biggest hug and kiss I'd ever seen. J made herself right at home, while fresh Brim and grits cooked on the stove. She stared at the high ceilings like a little baby. We had a great time watching J entertain Angelica. It was the happiest I'd seen her in years. I'll preserve that day in my heart forever because that was that last time that I beheld my grandmother.

The next week my grandmother, Jeadie M. Davis, passed away in her sleep. I had to be very strong, especially for daddy. J's death devastated him, and he began drinking. With no insurance, I assumed the total financial burden of her funeral and plunged deeper into debt. On December 2, 1992, I buried my grandmother at the Restlawn Cemetery in Jacksonville, Fl. Many friends and family grieved over our loss, but life would never be the same without her.

After J's death my life evolved totally into a spiritual journey. God clearly called me to a higher purpose, and I devoted my life totally to Islam, in spite of the wishes of others. Renita cringed whenever Farrakhan was mentioned; she had an askant perception of Islam. Others thought that I was crazy and had abandoned Jesus and everything he stood for. Thank God for my mother and father. They never crucified me for standing for what I believed.

I was plummeting into the abyss of hell, but the principles that were engrained within the religion of Islam, resurrected me to my highest fidelity, and I became a beacon of light. My eyes were opened to the terrible reality and injustice that was ruining America, especially among the poor black and oppressed people of this nation that were enslaved to false concepts and practices. No longer did I follow the religious traditions, like the many generations before me. Instead, I made a conscious decision based on study that I considered factual, mathematical, and practical. I saw racism, classicism, and sexism at the root of society's ills. The handwriting was on the wall; the country was becoming morally degenerate. There were millions of innocent people I saw in need of a word that would redeem, heal, and initiate the process of salvation. Therefore, I decided to use my popularity and dedicate my life to help Minister Farrakhan in this mission.

Over the next several months my life slowly transformed. I began by writing a letter to request the return of my slave name for a holy and righteous name that our fathers once had back in the east. Then, I studied night and day. I learned the scientific facts about the creation and history of the black man. The more I grew spiritually in the Mosque, the more Renita opposed my beliefs. Tension and strife invaded my home like a thief in the night. Renita and I were divided along religious lines of authority. I watched my marriage corrode as I fought an internal and external battle within my own home. Soon, Renita and I were totally disconnected from each other. I couldn't turn back if my life depended on it. My hunger and thirst for knowledge became irresistible. I watched videos of the Minister for hours, late into the night. I built a library composed of hundreds of tapes, videos, and books.

Later that year, I was called to assist Minister Eddie in the ministry. We traveled throughout the entire country aiding Minister Farrakhan. I learned a lot under Minister Eddie's tutelage. Each Sunday I opened the Mosque with Fahja prayer. Also, I visited local churches and schools, teaching and speaking the message of Islam as taught by the Honorable Elijah Muhammad. The Mosque became my second home. I attended F.O.I. (Fruit of Islam) classes for the men on Mondays, study night with the Quran was on Wednesdays, self-improvement class on Fridays,

Minister Elgin X, local representative for the Minister Louis Farrakhan and a businessman. — John Pemberton/el

and Mosque meetings on Sundays. There was little time for anything else, but I was closer to happiness than ever before.

Going to hear Minister Farrakhan preach rejuvenated my soul. Throngs of black people filled the auditorium, in record numbers, while protestors picketed outside. Despite the protestors, the events always ended in peace and love. However, the greatest experience was attending Saviors Day. On many occasions, my entire family attended along with me to celebrate the birth of Master Fard Muhammad, the Mahdi, and founder of the Nation of Islam. He was born February 26, 1877, in the Holy City of Mecca. Later that same year we honored the birth of the Honorable Elijah Muhammad on October 7, 1897, born in Sandersville, Georgia. It was in those two mighty men that our trust and faith were rooted. Minister Farrakhan boldly represented them. The highlight of my Muslim journey came as a shock when I was suddenly appointed the new Minister of the Muhammad Mosque in

Jacksonville, replacing my mentor and friend Minister Eddie. I worked feverishly to improve economic development and community relations with various religious organizations in the city. Our plans worked like a charm, as the Muslim community and the Ambassadors of Christ united and shared the same sanctuary. This gave hope to thousands that had become divided by religious barriers. The community was inspired by our act of unity and solidarity. However, some perceived it as blasphemy and attempted to disrupt the good intentions of the righteous. But prayer and hard work kept us moving forward, as we overcame one hurdle after another.

As my popularity increased, my job became more hectic. Slowly, I became an advocate for justice on behalf of the poor and weak. As a consequence, my father became my number one ambassador. Whether I was standing on the football field or behind the pulpit he always had my back. Before speaking I was always comforted by his loving smile. But nothing would have meant more than having my wife beside me. I needed her support more than ever.

Our relationship needed a miracle if we were to survive. That miracle came in the form of a baby girl. Renita gave birth to an angel on her birthday. Yasmeen Zaire Davis was born on November 15, 1994. Angelica was four years old and loved playing big sister. Sometimes she'd hold the bottle during feeding time or helped out with changing

diapers. Angelica loved her little sister; both of them made me proud. Renita and I began to rekindle our relationship.

I quit my day job and became an employee with the Jacksonville Sheriff's Office. Three months later I resigned and opened my own business.

On October 16, 1995, Minister Farrakhan called for a Million Man March in Washington D.C. The news sent shock waves across the nation and throughout the world as opinions ricochet. Some rejoiced, while others criticized the Minister and condemned the March. We had only a couple of months to organize, register voters, and finance the largest march in the history of America. It was a relentless sacrifice that involved various political and faith based organizations.

I worked day and night overseeing the local and daily operations while speaking in as many churches and colleges as possible. Frequently, I appeared on local TV and radio shows promoting the Million Man March. All throughout the nations various social, political, and religious organizations supported Minister Farrakhan by endorsing the march, especially BET. However, many angry serpents launched venomous attacks against the Minister and the march. Nevertheless, on October 16, 1995 the world witnessed nearly two million black men unite on the mall in Washington D.C. We petitioned Gods' forgiveness by atoning for all our past sins and transgressions. The Million Man March resulted in the most peaceful and powerful public demonstration in the history of America. I was one of the many millions that were truly blessed to see and experience an event of such magnitude. The Million Man March was a symbol of moral rectitude, and the ramifications affected millions around the globe.

On the week of the march, daddy and I, along with my friends Anthony and Herman finalized our travel plans to Washington D.C. I accepted a personal challenge along with all the Muslims around the country. As a sacrifice to God, we fasted for a week. Initially, I struggled with dizziness and severe stomach cramps. I craved for food, but I prayed for God's help. I fed my mind intellectually and spiritually by reading the Holy Quran. Soon, the pain and hunger subsided. Within days I had lost a considerable amount of weight and I was forced to tighten my belt in order to keep my pants from sagging around my waist. I became an empty vessel nourished only by the word of God. Soon, my complexion radiated, and my mental aptitude was sublime.

My fast elevated me closer and closer to God; it was my greatest accomplishment in life.

The next morning, we left town and headed to Washington D.C. The highways were congested with eager marchers. However, it was the greatest demonstration of peace and brotherhood. Banners and posters littered each vehicle, and friendly gestures were exchanged. Nevertheless, harsh rhetoric littered the airwaves condemning the messenger. We all prayed together and reflected on our commitment to become better men.

Soon, we arrived in the District of Columbia and assembled with marches at the Congressional Mall. A cool arctic breeze made the temperatures plummet near freezing. Tightly bundled under my coat, I helped the others assemble our tent. The mall became a sanctuary of peace and tranquility. Each man greeted his brother with love; it was heaven on earth. The entire world was focused on the Million Man March. News crews from around the world conducted interviews, giving the world a glimpse of our abnormity. Throughout the night the marchers arrived in groves, and the mall quickly began filling. With only hours before the event, I tried lying down on the cold frost bitten ground before assuming ministerial duties. But I tossed and turned. The constant pounding of vendors assembling their booths was too annoying.

With a restless night's sleep, I woke up in the dawning hour with my suit wrinkled and soiled. At 4:30AM I began my journey to the front of the mall for Fajah Prayer. Hundreds of F.O.I. marched in perfect caddice until they were assembled at the podium. Suddenly, the call for prayer resonant from the speakers; the call was heard for miles. Then different political, religious, youth leaders, gang leaders, and celebrities from around the world delivered messages of enlightenment. Quickly, the mall filled and many climbed into trees to assure themselves a peep into history. There was a sea of tranquility as far as the naked eye could see. Countless black men representing a diverse spectrum of unity made their way to the mall from all parts of the globe. The world saw a glimpse of heaven. The Minister eloquently addressed a wounded nation with a message of love and guidance. The message renewed our faith in God and each other. Millions joined hands in solidarity and pledged to become better men, husbands, and fathers. Soon, the tears began to fall like rain and black men embraced one another with love. It was a tender moment in history.

The Million Man March will always be revered in my heart as a divine experience. On my return home, my family greeted me admirably; they were extremely proud. However, my work as a minister had just begun. The Mosque overflowed with guests and converts, while national organizing communities fulfilled the political and spiritual agenda of the Million Man March. Local leaders opened their hearts and embraced my presence. The Million Man March had produced an ecumenical effect. Spiritual leaders from various denominations stood together in solidarity. Also, I noticed a tremendous change in daddy's faith; he put down the bottle and picked up the Bible. Even Renita's views concerning Islam appeared to have changed. It was a joy to feel loved and respected in spite of my beliefs.

But my favorite moments remained with my daughters. Angelica and Yassy were my darling angels; watching them grow up was the joy of my life. Often after a stressful day, the girls would greet me at the front door with a warm smile. Clinging to each leg they yelled, "Daddy!"

Slowly, I hobbled to the kitchen table with my brief case firmly gripped. Yassy cheerfully unlaced my shoes, while Angelica warmed my plate in the microwave. Their love for me made sacrificing for them a pleasure. Later, dad and I attended the Million Women's March in Philadelphia and the Million Family March with the girls back in Washington D.C. in 2000.

Within twelve months the mosque was decimated by an arsenal of media attacks. The attendance faltered, and seeds of discontentment were sewed. I was accused of misappropriation of funds. Shortly, a regional investigation was launched and I was temporarily suspended from any ministerial duties. I was deeply offended. The stress mounted and invaded my home. Heated arguments escalated and living with each other became a living nightmare. Soon, I questioned my faith, marriage, and life. Eventually, I resigned as the Minister of Muhammad Mosque. Later, Renita requested a divorce. I was devastated; especially when I thought about the girls. I lost two families that year, and I took my first drink of alcohol in nearly ten years.

Alien to my Muslim beliefs, I began living an undisciplined and adulterous lifestyle. Vicious rumors circulated, and I lived under scrutiny. I was lost without my family and took refuge under dad's wings. He encouraged me to live upright and to set a good example for the girls. I depended on dad's guidance to nourish me back to strength.

But there were many trials yet to come. The next day, dad was rushed to the hospital. He arrived complaining of severe stomach pains. When I arrived into his room, he was lying in bed unconscious. He had a catheter inserted into his penis, and multiple I.V.'s protruded from his veins. The doctors performed an emergency tracheotomy, and the wheezing sound of dad gasping for air was traumatizing. Frantically, I paced around the hospital searching for answers; but no one responded. Quickly, I rushed back into dad's room and prayed by his bedside. Suddenly, the doctor walked in with a stethoscope around his neck. He looked at me and said, "Your father is sick. I don't know if he's going to make it."

I was lost for words. I backed into a corner and stared angrily out of the window. The doctor explained that my father's colon had burst and his body was infected by fecal matter. Dad suffered from a potentially fatal disease called Diverticulitis. Dad's body was becoming more infected with each passing minute. He needed an antibiotic fast. Unfortunately, the culture test demanded a twenty-four hour turnaround; we didn't have that much time. The physician was forced to administer an alternative drug.

Meanwhile, the hospital prepared me for the worse, and suggested that I make final arrangements. But I remained by daddy's bed side until his vital signs began to improve. The next morning, surgery was performed to remove a part of his colon. Dad lay lifeless while I read the Bible aloud and prayed for him. There were encouraging signs that daddy could hear me; each night I wiped away tears from his eyes. Daddy's condition appeared stable, and just when I thought that I could breathe a sigh of relief, he developed a severe case of Pneumonia. He had a relapse and we were back to square one. My father needed a miracle; only God could help.

A couple of days later, I made my routine visit to the hospital and found dad resting peacefully. I approached his bedside and gently whispered into his ear, "I love you daddy."

Dad opened his eyes and said, "I love you too son."

It was a miracle. I shouted out, "Daddy!"

That was one of the happiest days of my life. From that day on, daddy referred to me as an angel.

Daddy was admitted into a nursery home for six weeks, and his recovery was arduous. First, he had to attend speech therapy because his words slurred. Later, he had physical therapy to regain coordination. Dad's journey was difficult; his pride impeded his progress. Frequent arguments erupted between dad and his nurses, and he refused to eat. Each day I prepared dad a home cooked meal with his favorite side dish. Slowly, his attitude changed and he had won the staff's hearts; he became their favorite patient.

Finally, after weeks of rehab, dad was ready to go home. With his suitcase packed and his walking cane nearby he sat in his wheelchair anticipating my arrival. Immediately, my presence was welcomed. The staff members festively greeted me and escorted me to dad's room with a cake in their hands. Daddy was deeply touched as his nurses hugged and kissed him goodbye. Tears escaped from his eyes. Nobly, he gathered his composure and sat proudly in his wheelchair as I rolled him out. The shiny waxed floor squeaked as I walked and made sharp turns to exit the building; dad never said a word. Suddenly, we had arrived at the end of our journey; we had reached the front door. I locked daddy's wheelchair and said, "Come on dad, it's time to go."

He reached for his cane and struggled to his feet. Quickly, I ran to his aid, but he shouted, "No! I got it!"

Slowly, he placed one foot in front of the other and walked towards the car. I was inspired by his determination. I had to adjust my lifestyle to accommodate his needs. He completely depended on me for his livelihood. I questioned if I'd survive carrying the burden completely on my shoulders. Dad was disabled and his bank account was dissolved. I was forced to support two households with a limited income. Dad didn't have medical insurance and his bills escalated to $200,000; we needed help.

It was extremely difficult to keep dad motivated. His spirit started to wither, especially when he was denied social security and disability. Angelica's and Yassy's unconditional love became his saving grace. The four of us were inseparable, and we loved taking getaways. Our favorite destination was Miami's South Beach; I treasured those experiences. Everyone was excited, especially Yassy. Constantly she asked granddaddy if we were in Miami yet. The funny thing about it was we were only five miles out of Jacksonville; she was so innocent and cute. Angelica giggled and ate sunflower seeds.

It was touching to see the girls holding their grandfather's hand

while walking into the store. We were greeted in Miami by a tropical oasis. Groves of coconut trees adorned the city. Our hotel was nestled on the seashore, and a warm ocean breeze tantalized our senses. We had found paradise!

Daddy had the time of his life. He sat near the pool wearing his favorite panama hat tilted to the side. The girls played in the pool until they were exhausted. Their joyful laughs made our hearts swelter. Memories like those got us through the difficult times. However, back home dad's living condition was deplorable. He turned the house into a boarding home to produce income. Some tenants slept on the floor with rolled up clothes underneath their heads as pillows. Dad slept on a used mattress in the living room; it sat on concrete blocks. Strange nocturnal traffic invaded his home in the wee hours of the night. Anything that wasn't nailed down was stolen. Dad needed constant attention to keep from becoming depressed over his dilapidating condition. Dad's severe drinking problem began to take its toll. His health swiftly declined; high blood pressure, kidney, and heart problems arose. But dad was unmotivated to take his medication; he had lost his will to live. He sat in his favorite chair inebriated with strands of gray hair protruding from his beard.

I hated the burden that was placed on me. We needed help and I didn't know where to turn. Dad began collecting used cigarette butts to sell to the other poor people in the neighborhood for a nickel or dime. Sometimes a cigarette that was barely smoked would bring in a quarter.

I couldn't believe people where living like this in the richest country in the world. Often, daddy's drinking vengeance resulted into alcohol poisoning, and the pungent odor of vomit lingered in the house. Soon, the house became a cesspool of filth, an infestation of rats and roaches invaded the house; the stench was unbearable.

Finally, dad's luck changed when I hired an attorney. He won his social security and disability appeal, and was awarded back pay for the previous year. However, his health became more of an issue. Dad missed many of his doctor appointments in order to drink and celebrate with strangers. Dad's money was going fast and so was my patience. I took over his financial affairs and became the father in the relationship. Soon, dad had purchased a phone. That saved me time and money because I didn't have to drive miles just to check on him anymore. Those simple improvements did wonders for his confidence, but the best was still yet to come. Dad surprised everyone and purchased a Cadillac Coupe Deville. Finally, dad had the independence he needed, which revived his manhood; I was very proud of him. A major burden was removed from my shoulders. I even took dad to Chicago with me for Saviors Day. It was daddy's first time flying on a plane. I thought for sure dad would be excited, but the lust for alcohol was too tempting for him to resist. Dad found his way back into the hospital for alcohol related symptoms. At that point I gave up, and turned things over to God; I had done my best. It was time to live my own life.

Strangely, I received a prophetic revelation from my spiritual brother. Michael Muhammad said, "The greatest honor that God can give you is to place the well-being of your parents in your care. He is demonstrating the road that you will have to travel in order to be successful. Every time he falls and gets up, the example is for you. It's your trial, not his, because he is winning his battle. What about you?"

I was too blind to see that life entailed getting knocked down, but daddy showed me how to get up. I am forever grateful to Brother Muhammad for those words because they strengthened and inspired me to help others like my dad. I worked feverishly to serve my community. Soon, I established the Elgin Davis Foundation to benefit at risk children.

To market the foundation I did the unthinkable. I came out of retirement to play for the arena football league. Like usual, I had to put my old hamstring to the test. Early one Saturday morning, I met with the team to run drills. I started with the 40 yard dash. I got as far as the 30 yard line before my hamstring tore and left me hopping off the field again. As a consequence, I served as a player consultant for the Jacksonville Tomcats. Eventually, they became one of my biggest sponsors.

I was thrilled to adopt the kids at the local Boys and Girls Club. The foundation sponsored over a hundred kids to attend each home football game. It was a blessing to see the smiles on their faces. With the help of the Orthodontic Center of America, I was able to provide braces and free teeth cleanings for the kids.

Many of the local and retired NFL players attended functions to support my cause. Our greatest event occurred during a "back to school" rally. Local radio stations aided my foundation with public service announcements and a live appearance in the A. Phillip Randolph Park. The Tomcat's mascot and cheerleaders came out and got the crowd excited about going back to school. It was an all-day event that attracted religious, political, and business communities together. The foundation supplied the children with hundreds of backpacks and school supplies for the upcoming year. However, the greatest memory occurred during a fund-raiser the Tomcats sponsored. It was a great event. Many showed their support by purchasing auctioned items. Dad told me that he was proud of me for what I was doing for the kids, and that God was going to bless me. That really meant a lot coming from daddy. On stage I thanked the Tomcats and my guests. Then, I noticed a little girl up front with Muscular Dystrophy. She wasn't older than four. I couldn't take my eyes off of her. Her smile was infectious. I walked towards her with tears in my eyes. Suddenly, I knelt down and gave her a kiss. Chills raced down my spine. I felt compelled to do something special for her, but unfortunate circumstances denied me the opportunity. Deeply, I apologize to you and your family little angel. I pray that you read this book and contact me. I have your gift.

I really enjoyed working and meeting with people associated with my foundation. It was my way of giving charity and an out-growth of my ministry. It was surely a blessing for many, but my personal needs beckoned my call and my foundation slowly faded away. Soon, I purchased a cleaning franchise in Jacksonville. It certainly was a challenge as I worked two years developing my business. Most weekends the girls and I rode to Orlando. We enjoyed Central Florida, especially Wet N' Wild and the Disney parks. I felt a sense of peace and freedom in Orlando. Often I considered relocating, but the thought of leaving daddy was preposterous.

However, my decision to relocate was persuaded by a charismatic salesman. I met Juan at a prestigious resort in Orlando. Juan showed me a luxurious three bedroom, three bathroom condo; it was immaculate. Immediately, I was sold on the concept of vacation ownership. It was ideal for my family; mom and dad would have loved it. Juan bragged about the industry and he encouraged me to change careers. The hours and the money were perfect; all I needed was a real estate license.

When I returned to Jacksonville I enrolled into the Watson School of Real Estate. I took a sixty-three hour course in one week. The class hours were from 8AM-5PM, but my day had only begun. From 7PM-3AM I managed my business. It was a tumultuous schedule, but I survived and successfully completed the course.

Surprisingly, daddy endorsed my decision to relocate to Orlando. He and the girls were excited about visiting the theme parks on the weekend. I was elated to have their support. However, mom appeared sad. But quickly she warmed up to the idea as time went by.

On June 30, 2003 my journey took me down a different path. I relocated to Orlando with two friends from real estate school, and joined a virgin company in the timeshare industry. Wyndham Palms Resort and Country Club was a cultivating experience. Quickly, I established myself as an asset for the company, and my coworkers found working with a former NFL player intriguing.

Life couldn't have been better. I was implored to visit Jacksonville on the weekends. Dad and the girls were becoming extremely close; they were inseparable. I was happy to see them showcase their love.

Daddy felt compelled to visit the nursing home just to say hello. He was greeted like a celebrity and everyone raved over his appearance. Abruptly, daddy's nurse came rushing towards us with tears in her eyes. She looked at my daddy and said, "Freddy, because of you, I know that

God has power. I hope he can heal me the way he healed you, because I have cancer."

Our hearts stopped beating, and dad embraced her into his arms. We both agreed that you must be careful about how you treat others when you're up, because you may need them when you're down. Dad was a blessing to many people that day.

While departing, I noticed a young lad playing recklessly in the park. I was a bit taken away; he was a frisky fellow. Suddenly, dad looked at me and said, "I use to know a little fellow just like that."

Later we went over to mom's house for dinner. The girls decorated the house with their spirit while dad ate his favorite dish. It was just like old times.

Mom said, "Freddy sit back and wipe your face. I want you to enjoy your food."

Humbly, he smiled and scooted back into his chair. He cleaned his plate and licked his fingers, then he requested seconds.

Mom laughed and said, "Golly Fred, you'll work a person to death!"

Dad still loved momma with all his heart. You could see

it in his eyes and hear it in his voice, but I knew there was no chance for them getting back together. However, I enjoyed entertaining the thought.

Saying goodbye was heartbreaking, but I had to take dad home and get back to Orlando. The girls gripped daddy's hand and patiently helped him out of the truck. When he arrived at the front door he hugged the girls and gave them an allowance.

The girls shouted, "Thank you Granddaddy. We love you!"

Granddaddy replied, "I love ya'll too. Do good in school and listen to your momma and daddy. See ya next time!"

Over the next several weeks I watched daddy return to the father I used to know. He stopped drinking and became more responsible with visions of returning back to church. Joyfully, I relinquished the father role back to my dad. To celebrate I planned a family vacation back to Asheville, North Carolina; it was my first time returning since I was a little boy. Dad was flabbergasted; he told all of his friends. It honored him in ways that I never expected. November 1, 2004 became our departure date. The foliage was beautiful in North Carolina that time of the year. With it only two weeks away, I made the final preparations.

On October 18, around noon, I experienced an eerie feeling. My head ached, and I drove to the mall for lunch. Before entering my cell phone rang. It was Debbie; she was a close family member that lived three houses from daddy. She sounded strange. Debbie asked me to sit down, because she wanted to talk to me about my father.

I replied, "Is he not feeling well?"

Debbie said, "No Elgin, your dad passed away earlier today."

The words penetrated my heart and pierced my soul. Oceans of tears emptied the burden of my afflictions, sending me into shock. Suddenly, my heart began beating uncontrollably. I dropped my cell phone and embraced myself with both arms. I was unable to talk. I stared into the heavens with my head tilted back and screamed, "Why God, why?"

I ran back to my truck and sat behind the steering wheel, panting and wiping away the dribble that fell from my mouth and nose. Suddenly, I became outraged and pounded on the steering wheel violently until I became fatigue. I tried calling mom but there was no answer. There was no one to help absorb my pain. I left Orlando with the clothes on my back.

The hardest part was driving home. Barely, I avoided running off the road; tears impaired my vision. I found myself blinking in and out, but the sounds of safety bumps guided me back to the center of the road. I felt lifeless, but somehow I found the fortitude to pray to God. As I drove to Jacksonville, I reminisced about the countless visits that I had made and the feeling of being embraced in the loving arms of my father. But this time I had no father to embrace. I drove within blocks of the house hoping this was all a dream and that I would wake up to find my father alive and well. The closer I drove to the house, the more my hopes and dreams of a miracle vanished. I saw daddy's stained mattress and sheets sitting on the side of the road. Slowly, I got out of my vehicle and walked into the house that sheltered, nourished, and sanctified my father and grandfather's spirit. I was the only living survivor. My dad's roommate sat on the porch crying and drinking a 40oz of beer. Moses told me that daddy departed around 11AM with his hands up surrendering. I walked from room to room thinking about the life that occupied these walls. I had precious and priceless memories.

Soon, the neighbors arrived and offered their condolences. Eventually, I walked over to Debbie's house and talked with Jack and Oretha. They loved my father unconditionally. Oretha relinquished $1,300 that belonged to dad. Then, she revealed a shocking revelation that occurred the night before. It confirmed where my father's spirit had ascended. Early that morning, around 3AM dad called Oretha acting hysterical. He was concerned about three men that he saw standing in his front door adorned in white. Unsure and frightened by their presence, he asked Oretha if she sent them over. Quickly, she dismissed the experience as a dream and told him to go back to sleep.

But he insisted, in a stern voice, that it wasn't a dream and hung up. Minutes later, he called back to inform Oretha that the strangers were still there. He confessed of being afraid. That was the last time Oretha had heard dad's voice.

Word had reached momma in Georgia and she drove back to Jacksonville as fast as she could to be at my side. While grieving, she catered to my needs. We both cried on each other's shoulder, especially when mom found out that the angels had arrived to deliver daddy's soul to God.

As tears rolled down her eyes, mom reflected on our last supper. She said, "I didn't realize that it was my last time seeing him alive. I would have served him as many plates as he wanted. But I didn't know son. That's why we must always treat people nice all the time while they're alive. I just didn't know."

I had five days to prepare the funeral and deal with the emotional loss of my father. I didn't know where to start. I had inherited a financial burden. Mom and I arrived at the funeral home and picked out an affordable casket. I tried to maintain my composure, but emotional outbreaks occurred without warning. But mom held my hand and consoled me. Over the next few days we contacted friends and family to inform them of our loss. I packed up all of dad's clothes and valuables into a box and dusted off the cobwebs from the cracked picture frames that proudly displayed majestic memories.

On October 23, 2004 scores of sympathizers gathered at the First Baptist Church of Oakland to offer their respect to the deceased. It was a wonderful ceremony. The soulful rhythms of the church choir soothed the ailing hearts of the distressed. I sat in the front row with my family and mourned. Gently, mom nudged me and offered her handkerchief. Soon, an usher rushed to my aid to offer support. Softly she messaged my shoulders until I was composed. Before the eulogy I walked towards the microphone to give a final tribute to my father. I unsettled a lump from my throat and dried my eyes. I noticed faces in the audience that I hadn't seen in years. Suddenly, I glanced at the girls for strength. Somehow I delivered an electrifying speech that spawned a barrage of emotions that culminated into an endless river of tears. But the most difficult struggle was yet to come. At the grave site I realized that I would never see my father again. Renita embraced me while tears rolled down my face. I stared at my father lying in the casket. He was nobly dressed in a gray pin-striped suit. Dad had a peaceful look on his face. Then, I gently caressed his face with my hand; his body was cool and damp. Finally, I reached around my neck and unlocked the safety pin from my gold Patriot necklace; it symbolized my greatest trophy, and proudly placed it into dad's right hand. Renita assured me with a hug that dad was in a better place. I waited alone and watched dad's casket slowly being lowered into the earth; it was painful to watch. Patiently, my family waited for me in the limousine parked up front. After one last glimpse and a final goodbye I walked towards the limo with my head down, feeling numb and lifeless. I found breathing as difficult as burying my father. I watched the dirt as it covered my dad's casket from the window while the limo drove away. Suddenly, I requested that the driver return to the grave site so I could be with my dad one last time. I got out and walked alone to be with my daddy until the casket was covered. Unexpectedly, Renita approached me with her arms wide and makeup running from her eyes. We stood together for the first time in years. I thanked her for being there for me and my father through the rough and difficult times. She never complained and loved him like her own father. I told her that I will always love her for that. We waited together until the last grain of dirt fell on daddy's coffin. Finally, I received closure.

Immediately, I returned to mom's house for the recession, and my family and loved ones sang Happy Birthday to me. On October 23, 2004 I chose to celebrate life and live in honor of my father.

Fred Edward Davis was buried on my 39th birthday. He was laid to rest at the Restlawn Cemetery in Jacksonville, Fl at the age of 64.

Fred Edward Davis

June 4, 1940 – October 18, 2004

Rest in Peace

SUMMARY POINTS

It's been several years since daddy passed. But I thank God everyday for the gift of life and my unique experiences, starting with my parents whom God chose to introduce me to life. Therefore I will always be in debt to God for his grace, mercy, and love. God has proven to me that he'd never abandon me, and I'm learning how to love him more. For anyone who may be facing a struggle in their life, know that storms don't last forever. If you will trust in God and resist the temptation that comes along with the need of relieving affliction, then you will grow and qualify for a higher blessing. All undeserved suffering is redeemable.

Kids, please respect, honor, and obey your parents, even if you feel that your parents are unworthy. They gave you life, and that's the greatest gift anyone can receive, no matter what circumstances surround that life.

Please believe in your destiny and purpose. Your birth into the world is proof that there is something great in life for you to do. Your challenge is to discover you gift, cultivate it, and serve humanity. May God bless you in your quest! To those that desire to excel in athletics, nothing replaces hard work and dedication. You don't need steroids and other illegal substances to excel. You must be patient and continue to dream. I know that with millions on the line in today's sports industries the need to gain any advantage may appear to be irresistible, but the potential health risks are too great. Alarmingly, the average life span among NFL players is only 58 years of age. Even something as harmless as Cortisone can be deadly. Look at what happened to me. The drug permanently damaged my hamstring and ended a great NFL future. I was robbed of millions which could have changed my life and the people that I loved. The serious side effects exposed me to diabetes and heart related illnesses. My brothers and sisters, professional sports are businesses and you must always remember that you're only as good as your last performance. When your prime has passed and your performance falters, you become dispensable like those before you. The doctors and team physicians work on the owner's behalf, not yours. Their job is to keep teams from losing money on their investment (you). Many will do whatever it takes to get you back on the field making money for them; even if it means pumping your body with Cortisone at half time to get you back on the field. Remember that there's a life after football. The question is what happens to you after the fans and the bright lights are gone?

To the owners of the various professional teams, it's vital that you provide an exit program to support and help the former players adjust to the pain and hurt of untimely ending careers. Too many athletes are wounded mentally, physically, and psychologically; resulting in divorces, alcoholism, drug addiction, and even suicide. There are thousands of athletes that feel this way and go unrepresented, betrayed and abandoned. This insensitive act of abandonment must end. This is the dim reality of life in the NFL. The average NFL player's career lasts only three and a half years. The door revolves so regularly because of pensions that are earned if the players survive for four years. And to keep from paying pensions, most teams dispose of players that may be borderline, especially if health becomes a major issue, as in my case. (Remember, the NFL is a business first!)

The best remedy for you my friends is to invest in a quality education. That's the only true guarantee to a successful life. Next, build your spiritual character with some faith based religion. You will need Godly morals and principles to become truly successful in this world. While striving for success, please remember to always treat people the way you want to be treated.

To young adults, the lust for material possessions has ruined our society. The need to lie, steal, cheat, and murder are common practices among our youth. Too many senseless deaths have occurred and robbed families of their loved ones because we didn't have the fortitude, patience, or love for human life. Selling drugs has become a way to make easy money, leaving only two options, death or imprisonment. This has become the fate of too many of our youth. But if you seek ye first, the Kingdom of Heaven, all things will come. See, the Kingdom of Heaven is above; and the highest place you can ascend. You must seek the high things in life, such as truth, patience, love, and knowledge. Those will earn you all the material things you want, and more!

Next, honor the sacred vows of your marriage to ensure a fruitful and happy union. Be good companions to each other, and always be fair, kind, and respectful to one another. Family is the basic building blocks to a healthy nation. We must preserve the sanctity of the home; it's our saving grace. Parents please encourage your children and support their dreams with your time, sacrifice, and guidance. This does wonders for their confidence and self-esteem.

Please dear family, never use or abuse our elderly. Let's respect and help make their last days on Earth the greatest. Finally, to those who have lost family members and loved ones, such as I have, I pray that you find joy in your heart when reflecting on the precious memories that were left behind. May God heal any void in your heart. Life has been an adjustment without my dad. Some days I cry, and other days I reflect on the memories and smile. But I always thank God for blessing me with the kindest and the most loving father anyone could have. I wish you could have known him. Also, I thank God for a beautiful mother. She is the rose of my heart, and one of God's greatest works of perfection.

Therefore, I stand as their witness and I offer their example to the world. Thank you for honoring me, my family, and all of those that God has used to affect my life. We would like to encourage you to fight the good fight and walk the good walk until we see you again!

Peace and Blessings!

APPENDIX

Today's professional athletes are paid millions and loom larger than life. Their lavish lifestyles go beyond comprehension and attract a plethora of controversy, including drugs, money laundering, illegal gambling, and even murder. However, none is more polarizing than steroids.

Sports fans witnessed the degenerative effect steroids had on Los Angeles Raider Lyle Alzado; eventually resulting in his death. Olympic sprinter Ben Johnson was stripped of his Gold metal and baseball legend Barry Bonds reputation goes without honor due to the use of steroids. No matter the sport, the underlying motivation is the same, money. Nearly half of all athletes will take some form of steroids throughout their career to relieve pain, increase performance, or prolong their careers; especially with millions on the table. Many athletes only see the immediate gratification of fortune and fame. However, few have the maturity or guidance to see the long term side effects of steroids.

Some steroids have greater health risks than others. Anabolic steroids increase muscle mass, endurance, speed, and strength. Its illegal use could alter the outcome of competitive competition. This unfair advantage has probed strict investigations by league officials. Those that are brave enough to risk losing their careers and reputations suffer severe consequences, including suspensions, fines, and public ridicule.

Cortisone is currently un-prohibited and unregulated. Few critics have exposed its use and serious side effects.

Cortisone is in a family of medicines called Corticosteroids, which are strong anti-inflammatory drugs designed to reduce swelling, consequently relieving pain from the joints, tendons, or bursa. The Corticosteroids medicine is usually mixed with a local anesthetic and then injected into the painful area. The shot may feel uncomfortable, but the anesthetic helps alleviate the discomfort. In most cases, the cortisone will reduce the inflammation and subside pain within two to three days. However, repeated shots can lead to a number of serious side effects, including weight gain, osteoporosis, reduced immunity, increased risk of infection, and long term damage to an inflamed joint or tendon. These risks coupled with the fact that the shots don't have any curative effect on the underlying problem make them a poor choice for long term treatment. As a result, many professional athletes have filed lawsuits against teams. Dick Butkus, the Hall of Fame linebacker of the Chicago Bears, became the first pro-athlete to successfully sue and receive compensation. He alleged that repeated injections of cortisone from the team doctor put his long term health at risk.

If sports related injuries escalate your best option is to consider whether your injury is a result of a weakness or improper training and address those possibilities. Among the alternatives you can explore acupuncture, osteopathic manipulation, natural anti-inflammatory, or rest.

Reference web-sites:

www.drugs.com/MTM/cortisone.html

www.prolonews.com/knee_cortisone_prolotherapy_hauser.htm

www.geocities.com/bigcory94533/alzado.html

ABOUT THE AUTHOR

Elgin Davis, a native Floridian, was born on October 23, 1965 in Jacksonville, Fl. At an early age he learned life principles from his family's strong spiritual beliefs and humble roots. His unique gifts and talents earned him respect and honor among his community and peers. Quickly, Elgin established himself as a leader on and off the field, and received many accolades in high school, including President of Christian Athletes, captain of the football and track teams, and recognition from America's Outstanding Names and Faces. His tenacity on the football field earned him recognition as one of the state's top football prospects and he was bestowed the athlete of the year in high school. He attended the University of Central Florida on a full athletic scholarship. During his junior and senior year he was a Dean's List recipient and voted captain of the football team. Elgin evolved into the most prolific runner in school history. In 1987, Elgin Davis was drafted into the NFL by the New England Patriots, and became the second player ever drafted out of UCF. There, he played two seasons before signing with the Pittsburgh Steelers and later the Winnepeg Blue Bombers of the CFL. He ended his career with the London Monarchs of the World Football League. Shortly afterwards, Elgin answered the call of ministry, and worked diligently within his community to help correct many political and social ills that affect society. Today, he resides in Orlando, Fl and works in real estate.

LaVergne, TN USA
01 September 2009
156626LV00001B/20/P